Matt 5:16
Light
Shine ✶

Zip-a-Dee-Doo-Dah
Zip a day
My O my what a wonderful day
Plenty of sunshine coming my way
heading

Mr. Blue
On my Shoulder
It's the truth
It's actual
everything
is satisfactual
Zip-a-Dee Doo-Dah

~~2064~~ Pinochio 1940
When You Wish Upon
A Star

Cinderella –
Bibbidi-Bobbidi Boo

Mary Poppins – supercali
fragilistic expialidocious
#76 Song of the

Academy Award
South
Zip
Zip

Quietly Zip
Removed Aug 26
2s 2s

Wonderful day
Wonderful Feeling Feeling This way

"The gospel of Jesus Christ is meant not only to deliver our souls to heaven but also to transform our behavior on earth. And, deeper still, it is meant to transform our desires, our attitudes, and our instincts. It is even meant to transform our reactions and responses to those who oppose us, disagree with us, or sin against us. In this timely book, Paul Tripp calls us to react to the chaos around us in a distinctly Christian way that counters the toxicity that exists deep within our hearts and deep within our culture. If we would heed his call, the world would be blessed, the church would be strengthened, and the Savior would be glorified."

Tim Challies, author, *Seasons of Sorrow: The Pain of Loss and the Comfort of God*

"*Reactivity* offers a rich gospel perspective for navigating relationships with Christlikeness. The practical applications paint a hopeful picture of what could be if we let God's word transform us. A must-read for anyone engaging with others online!"

Ruth Chou Simons, *Wall Street Journal* bestselling author; artist; Founder, GraceLaced Co.

"In this helpful and timely volume, Paul provides us with a much-needed blueprint for the use of technology that not only avoids sin but also advances truth, beauty, goodness, and love in an otherwise hostile space. I can't recommend *Reactivity* highly enough."

Scott Sauls, Senior Pastor, Christ Presbyterian Church; author, *Jesus Outside the Lines* and *Beautiful People Don't Just Happen*

"Every day we find ourselves walking through a minefield of online rage. But now our friend Paul Tripp helps us turn from that 'culture of toxic reactivity' toward a community of life-giving response to Jesus. What could be more attractive—or urgently needed?"

Ray Ortlund, President, Renewal Ministries

"Paul David Tripp says that logging off Twitter won't get you away from angry reactivity. The polarizing way we communicate has seeped from social media into our families, our communities, and our churches. With wisdom and grace, Tripp lays a path from frustrated reactivity to gospel-centered communication. While this book would benefit anyone, I'd especially recommend it to any Christian leader on social media."

Sarah Eekhoff Zylstra, Senior Writer and Faith-and-Work Editor, The Gospel Coalition

"We communicate as much through our thumbs as with our lips, and with that come both unprecedented opportunities and dangers. Paul Tripp guides us with profound wisdom and insight. It's hard to think of anyone who wouldn't benefit greatly from reading this."

Sam Allberry, pastor; author, *What God Has to Say about Our Bodies*

"In an age of harried and often thoughtless engagement through social media, Paul Tripp offers us a gospel pause. He gets the reader to stop and reflect on a Christian's witness through our social platforms. I am so grateful for this resource and pray that the Lord would use it to foster wisdom for Christians to be salt and light in this world of unwise reactivity."

John Perritt, author; Director of Resources, Reformed Youth Ministries; host, *The Local Youth Worker* podcast

"Paul David Tripp offers not only an accurate and sobering diagnosis of our day, but also a hope-filled treatment plan so that we might get better. Tripp rightly addresses the church—the rage is not just out there, it's in here too. And he rightly reminds us of the gospel. By the end of the book I felt a renewed peace in our good and sovereign God, as well as a renewed drive to honor the Lord online, in person, and in my own heart."

Jen Oshman, author, *Enough about Me* and *Cultural Counterfeits*

[Handwritten margin notes:]

Spiritual... Spiritual health... lack...

you are more than your feelings and thoughts — Spiritual open hearted — full open hearted — 2 things!

and meaningfull and look and forth - active nature

136
99
88
29

Ps 32:7

- alive -
- protecting bond
amazing bond

GOD } Among Normal?! Active Spirit
↳ us } ~Transformation~
Miserable
Theories of ?   John 13:34

Twist CR Theory   I John 4:9
                       Phil 1:6
Al Gore | Green
Bill Gates ?   Y ⟵ Mercy
a   b   ⟵ Grace
Carbon Neutral
Away to Make   So Respond   Get
&   So Fast   Out of It

reactivity

··· { Victorious }   ··· Clue less ···
    { Women }   Spirited ~SWAMP~
mean Vicious   or
                           Let's

                       New Focus
Common   Enter-
ground   Prayer   tain ?
Simplicity of
of Normal Unity   In Name of God
                       -N-F-L-Let It Be-

A ① thought "don't lo"being ···
· intimate thoughts ··· action
engaging playful
··· intelectual player ···

tension ··· laluru ···
– edge of understanding
         Truth
– The Trade of Love
Knowledge guns hugs
   ↑   ↑
   Kindness

Care giver – roll
all my life

Now ~ indipendent-
feed back

When you ——— · ° °
I Feel ——— · ° °
Accept Evolve –
Need X-Y-Z L

Other Books by Paul David Tripp

reactivity

How the Gospel Transforms
Our Actions and Reactions

Paul David Tripp

WHEATON, ILLINOIS

Cover design: Jordan Singer
First printing 2022
Printed in the United States of America

Hardcover ISBN: 978-1-4335-8266-0
ePub ISBN: 978-1-4335-8269-1
PDF ISBN: 978-1-4335-8267-7
Mobipocket ISBN: 978-1-4335-8268-4

Library of Congress Cataloging-in-Publication Data
Names: Tripp, Paul David, 1950– author.
Title: Reactivity : how the gospel transforms our actions and reactions / Paul David Tripp.
Description: Wheaton, Illinois : Crossway, 2022. | Includes bibliographical references and index.
Identifiers: LCCN 2022002644 (print) | LCCN 2022002645 (ebook) | ISBN 9781433582660 (hardcover) | ISBN 9781433582677 (pdf) | ISBN 9781433582684 (mobipocket) | ISBN 9781433582684 (epub)
Subjects: LCSH: Emotions—Religious aspects—Christianity. | Christianity and culture. | Christianity—Psychology.
Classification: LCC BV4597.3 .T75 2022 (print) | LCC BV4597.3 (ebook) | DDC 248.4—dc23/eng/20220617
LC record available at https://lccn.loc.gov/2022002644
LC ebook record available at https://lccn.loc.gov/2022002645

Crossway is a publishing ministry of Good News Publishers.

LSC	31	30	29	28	27	26	25	24	23	22
15	14	13	12	11	10	9	8	7	6	5	4	3	2	1

To the best ministry team ever. You are dedicated, faithful, and smarter than me. I am blessed that God sent you my way and that I get to walk this ministry journey with you.

Contents

Introduction

I AM NOT A TRAINED cultural critic or a digital media analyst, but I deeply believe that it is always helpful to look at whatever we are facing within ourselves, inside the Christian community, and in the surrounding culture through the lens of Scripture and the particular lens of the gospel. It is this discipline that has guided every book I have written. With each book I am asking the question "What would this thing look like if I were to view it from the vantage point of the gospel?" For most people the gospel is a means of past justification and future destination. Gloriously, the gospel is both of these things, but it also provides for us, right here, right now, a way of seeing, a means of interpreting, a guide to understanding, and a way of living. The truths of the gospel, its comfort, and its call give us a brand-new way of understanding and dealing with everything in our lives. The gospel is the gracious gift of the one who promised to give us everything we need not just for eternal life but also for godliness, that is, a God-honoring life between the time he takes us as his own and the time we go home to be with him.

It is important to remember that your Bible is comprehensive and not exhaustive. It does not tell you everything about everything. If your Bible were exhaustive, you'd have to transport it in five 18-wheelers to church on Sunday. There are many things the Bible is not a source of information for. But your Bible is comprehensive; while not telling you everything about everything, it gives you a lens through which to look at everything. It is with this understanding that I have written this book. I am giving you everything you need to understand our present culture, particularly our social media culture. The purpose of this book is to look at the culture of toxic reactivity, which seems to touch all of us daily, through the lens of the gospel. When we look at the dominant themes in our culture this way, we find understanding, clarity, calling, new direction, and hope. I have spent my life unpacking the glory, beauty, and depth of the gospel. This is the lane that God has called me to, and I plan on staying in that lane until I'm on the other side.

We live in the boisterous noise of a confusing world of thousands of voices. In the din of the noise, it's hard to hear yourself think. And with the power of digital media, it is nearly impossible to escape the cacophony and have enough quiet to meditate and evaluate. We carry a little device in our pockets or in our purses that connects us to thousands of opinions on thousands of topics every single day. Self-appointed influencers tell us how we should think and how we should react. No topic, no matter how small or how deeply significant, is left untouched. It seems as if everybody has something to say about everything. This creates confusion, and confusion is not a healthy or safe state of being.

We desperately need something in our lives that can cut through the noise of all the opinions, help us to think correctly, and respond appropriately to the things that we are now facing and will face down the road. I love how God speaks of his own truth in Proverbs 1:

To know wisdom and instruction,
    to understand words of insight,
to receive instruction in wise dealing,
    in righteousness, justice, and equity;
to give prudence to the simple,
    knowledge and discretion to the youth—
Let the wise hear and increase in learning,
    and the one who understands obtain guidance,
to understand a proverb and a saying,
    the words of the wise and their riddles.
The fear of the LORD is the beginning of knowledge;
    fools despise wisdom and instruction. (Prov. 1:2–7) [2]

Let me unpack what God says his truth is and what it is meant to do for us. First, God wants us to know that his truth is *practical* at a real-life level. It is meant to impact and shape your everyday living ("instruction in wise dealing," "the one who understands obtains guidance"). He wants you to know that his truth sets a *moral framework* by which you can evaluate anything ("instruction in . . . righteousness, justice, and equity"). He wants you to know that his truth *meets the needs of everyone* ("prudence to the simple, knowledge and discretion to the youth—Let the wise hear and increasing in learning"). And he wants you to know that his word helps you to *understand mysteries* you would not otherwise understand ("to understand a proverb and a saying, the words of the wise and their riddles"). This is what a biblical/gospel lens is meant to do for you as you grapple with the issues that press in on you every day.

This book is not a wide-ranging scientific or sociological examination of this current cultural moment, but it will ask us to put on our gospel glasses and take a look at the character and tone of the conversations that are taking place among us in person and, in a more focused way, on the media sites that we participate in daily. My hope is that looking at *what* we are saying to one another and *how* we are saying it through the lens of the gospel will not just inform us but will also convict and transform us, so as a gospel community we will stand above the toxicity that seems to be everywhere around us and shine as a city on a hill in a sadly darkened world.

1

Reactivity

I POSTED MY FIRST TWEET in February of 2009. I had been watching the rise of the internet and then the rise of what we now call social media. As I watched, it became clear to me that the way the human community connected and communicated was about to go through a seismic period of change. I thought that these new, internet–based media could be powerful tools for the gospel of Jesus Christ. I determined that I would post nothing but the gospel (except for my fun personal Instagram page). Over thirteen thousand tweets later, I still get up each morning, sit in the family room of our loft, and tweet three gospel thoughts. I will do this as long as I am able because, without leaving my chair, I can touch people all around the world with the gorgeous truths of the person and work of Jesus Christ and I can help them connect those truths to their daily living. Literally millions and millions of people have been touched by the gospel from my chair in that little room in Philadelphia. What stunningly powerful tools have been placed in our hands!

But there's a problem with tools. The hammer that can be used to build a house can also be used to smash a window in a robbery. The screwdriver that can be used to assemble something useful can be used to stab someone in a fit of anger. So it is with social media. Twitter today is not the Twitter of 2009. I am again and again shocked at the darkness that now lives there. Much of that darkness is in the way that people communicate with one another behind the protective cover of a remote screen and keyboard. I never post anything but the gospel and its call for our daily living, but I have had the ugliest responses, often slandering my beliefs, character, and motives. I have been told that I am a Marxist, that I have forsaken the gospel, and even that I am no longer a Christian.

Often it is evident in the disrespectful things that people have posted about me that people have not read the full post. They have reacted to a title or an opening line. It's a hair-trigger response that has become all too normal. Because it is a quick reaction, the communication is accusatory, unloving, and ungodly, and the content is largely unhelpful. I try my best to live as a humble student of the things of God. I don't think I am beyond the need for correction. I know that I have many things yet to learn. I deeply believe in the essential sanctifying ministry of the body of Christ. I believe that my faith, and the theology that delineates it, is a community project. I think loving correction is a grace. But the communication of disgust helps no one. Disrespectful responses seldom contribute to good things in the life of the receiver. These kinds of reactionary responses not only dishonor the receiver; they dishonor God. How can your heart not break when you read the ugly, dismissive, disrespectful, and accusatory responses to posts of wise and godly men and women?

The Twitter that I saw as a wonderfully powerful tool for gospel good is now talked about as a cesspool, a dark and abusive place.

There's even new lingo to capture that darkness. A person who attacks good, well-meaning people with abusive responses is known on social media as a "troll." And sadly, there are a whole lot of trolls out there. This reactionary darkness is so great that my friends in ministry often feel the need to take a Twitter break, that is, to separate themselves for a time from the darkness. Reactions without wisdom, reactions not shaped by love, reactions devoid of respect, reactions not tempered by honest self-examination, reactions that are more judgmental than corrective, reactions fueled by pride not humility, and reactions driven more by emotion than thoughtful reflection never produce anything godly and good.

But sadly, the culture of reactivity is not limited to social media. Consider our present political culture. It seems as though the days of thoughtful, respectful civil discourse are gone. The cooperative spirit, fueled by dignity and respect, that is necessary for politics and government to work seems either dead or taking its last gasps. Political figures seem better at yelling invectives at one another than they are at engaging in dignified and productive debate. The 2016 Republican nomination process alone should have left all of us shocked and saddened. The reactive ugliness on stage after stage was an embarrassment to the democracy we say we hold dear. While Democrats and Republicans call one another names, it is very hard for the work they are supposed to be doing on behalf of the citizens they represent to get done. If character really does matter in politics and government, then the prevalence of this ugly reactivity should grieve and concern us.

But the thing that has initiated the writing of this book is the presence of this reactivity culture in another essential domain. Sadly, this disruptive and dysfunctional culture of communication has infected and stained the church of Jesus Christ. When Jesus was in his final moment of tender instruction of his disciples, words meant to prepare them for a life of faith after his ascension, he said this: "By this all people will know that you are my disciples, if you have love for one another" (John 13:35). Let these words sink in. Jesus is saying that the mark of a disciple, the core indication that you have been visited, rescued, and transformed by grace, is not your theological prowess, your quick wit, your ability to win an argument, the success of your ministry, the number of your followers, your skill at getting clicks, how well you can put a person in his place, or the force of your communication. No, it's this one thing: love.

Love of others is not natural for us. Because of the selfism of sin, humble people-helping and God-honoring love is always the result of divine intervention. As John says, the reason we have any ability whatsoever to love one another is because we have first been loved by God (1 John 4:19). John even goes so far as to say this: "Beloved, let us love one another, for love is from God, and whoever loves has been born of God and knows God. Anyone who does not love does not know God, because God is love" (1 John 4:7–8).

Since God *is* love, everyone who knows God and is walking in communion with him should have a life that is characterized by love. Stop for a moment, put this book down, get out your Bible, and read 1 John 4. John's argument for the motivational centrality of love in the life of each one of God's children could not be stronger. Do you carry this central mark of discipleship? Is everything you say shaped by it? Is every reaction you make tempered by it? Is it the character quality you are known for? Do you make your point known, but at the expense of love? Do you react without taking the time necessary to have that reaction shaped by love? Does a quick-witted putdown motivate you more than a humble, patient, gentle, and loving response? Many of us are reacting in a way that falls way below the standard set for us in 1 John 4.

So many of the dark reactions on Twitter that I wrote about earlier were sadly from a Christian to another Christian. Daily I read responses by Christians to posts that are devoid of love—harsh, harmful, self-aggrandizing daggers, sent with little regard for the damage they do to the writer, the reader, and the reputation of the people of God. But I want to emphasize again that this lack of love is not just part of social media culture; we see this lack of love in the everyday reactions in the body of Christ.

I regularly mentor fourteen young men in ministry, with whom I meet individually. I think this may be the most important work I am doing right now. Each time I walk to meet with one of my guys, I am filled with a sense of the honor of what I am doing. That I have been chosen by God to do this work and that I have anything at all to offer these men argues for the power of God's intervening and transforming grace. In my conversations with these wonderful men, I have heard story after story of the ugly and disrespectful responses they have received from people they have endeavored to love and serve. But what has most shocked, concerned, and saddened me is that many of those unloving reactions came by way of a text, written in the middle of the pastor's sermon. Think about this. The person wasn't even willing to have his response tempered by the rest of the sermon. The writer didn't take time to consider what it would be like for the pastor to see the text not long after pouring his heart out in preaching.

Pastor after pastor has talked to me about dreading Monday morning emails, where all too often their motives, theology, or character is questioned because of one thing they said in a sermon, one announcement that was made, one conversation in the aisle, or some other thing that he did or did not do during or after a Sunday gathering. One pastor said to me, "Monday is the hardest day for me, not just because Sunday is emotionally and physically exhausting, but because of the emails and texts I get from the people that I love and serve." Whenever I hear a pastor say this, playing in the background are the words of Jesus, "By this shall all people know that you are my disciples." Of course, every pastor is a person in the middle of his own sanctification and is less than perfect. Of course, every pastor at some point will say and do wrong things. Of course, every young pastor has areas in his heart, communication, character, and conduct where he needs to mature. Of course, every pastor is a member of the body of Christ and, like everyone else, needs its ministry in order to grow. But there is still no place for dark, reactionary, disrespectful, judgmental, and harm-producing responses to him and his ministry.

I am afraid this reactionary culture also lives in our homes, where often our responses to one another are more shaped by stirred-up emotions than by humble, forgiving, and patient love. In our homes, flashes of irritation, anger, hurt, and impatience propel way more of our responses to one another than we are willing to admit. Let's be honest: it's not unusual for the communication between husbands and wives to be reactive rather than constructive. These responses lack biblical thoughtfulness, they're formed more by emotion than contemplation, and they provide more heat than light. The same is true with parenting. It is so easy as parents to react emotionally in ways that are unhelpful and surely don't advance the crucial work of heart transformation that our children need.

Here is the concern of this book. Reactivity is not new; you can trace it back to the garden of Eden. What is new is that this way of responding has become more and more normalized. I am afraid that we have gotten used to what Twitter and other social media sites have become. We have often passively accepted the denigration of our political discourse. Pastors have gotten used to the shots they regularly take as congregation members react to them and their ministry work. Much of our family talk would create a lot of embarrassment for us if played in public. We cannot, we *must not*, normalize a reactivity culture that is more of a culture of harm than a culture of grace. I need you and you need me, but if we keep slugging one another, sooner or later we're going to quit talking. This devolution of communication and its impact on relationships, which the Bible tells us are essential to God's ongoing work of rescue and transformation, are not okay.

By the power of God's amazing grace, we can do better. So, I want to begin by naming things in our responses to one another that we cannot allow to be normalized, and then for the rest of the book I want to propose a better way. In many ways, what I am going to propose is not new because it has its roots in the ancient wisdom of the word of God and its central theme, the gospel of Jesus Christ.

Don't Normalize What God Would Call Abnormal

God has made it clear that the norm for his children should be love. It is the thing that the listening and watching world should know us for. We should be recognized not only for the purity of our theology but also for the consistency of our love. This love is the new commandment that Jesus left with his disciples in his final days with them: "that you love one another: just as I have loved you, you also are to love one another" (John 13:34). The standard for our responses to one another is not just some standard of cultural niceness or human love. The standard is nothing less than the generous, sacrificial, pure, forgiving, and faithful love that God has so graciously showered down on us in the person of his Son.

Now, I will speak for myself here: this kind of love is not natural for me. If I am going to live out what God has chosen to be the norm for his children, then I need to start by confessing how utterly foreign this kind of love is for me and cry out for his rescuing and transforming grace. You see, I don't so much need to be delivered from the people around me who seem hard to love and be transported to some community populated by easier-to-love people. No, I need to be rescued from me, because until our Lord returns I will continue to be a flawed person, living near and relating to flawed people in a fallen world. In the world that I have just described, God's norm is only ever the result of the powerful operation of his grace.

So, because of the clarity of his call to love and his promise to us of empowering grace, there are things that we cannot allow to be normalized in our everyday responses to one another.

1. The normalization of emotionally driven responses. In our middle-of-our-sanctification imperfection, we will be hit powerfully with compelling and motivating emotions. Sometimes it will be hurt, sometimes fear, sometimes irritation, sometimes anger. If you go where those emotions lead you, you will do and say things that you should not do or say. So, if you want to live out the kind of responses God has called you to, you have to be good at saying no. I don't mean a cancel culture "no" to other people. What I mean here is saying no to yourself. Saying no to where that spontaneous anger is leading you, no to where fear may lead you, and no to the hurt that often makes you want to inflict hurt on others. How can you do this? God knew that between the "already" and the "not yet" your struggle with remaining sin would be so great that he did more

"already, not yet"

than just promise you forgiveness. God got inside of you by his Spirit. The Spirit that lives inside of you blesses you with the power to say no to where raging emotions may lead you and to turn and go in another, more restrained and loving direction. What would otherwise be impossible for you is made possible by the Spirit's presence and power, and that is a very good and encouraging thing.

2. The normalization of anger-driven responses. Although I talked about anger above, I want to give it added attention. It doesn't take very careful observation to conclude that we are living in an angry culture. Outrage of some kind, directed at someone who has created some offense somehow and needs to pay in some way, greets us every day. The level of hair-trigger intolerance of even minor foibles, errors, or offenses should concern us all. We are mad, and we are about to let you know it. Be very careful of what you post or say, because there are a lot of angry readers and listeners out there who are ready to respond with vengeance.

As I have reflected on the angry state of things, the words of James have come back to me again and again: "Know this, my beloved brothers: let every person be quick to hear, slow to speak, slow to anger; for the anger of man does not produce the righteousness of God" (James 1:19–20). May we be those who are known for being ready to listen, slow to speak, and not given to quick angry reactions.

3. The normalization of disrespectful responses. The level of cruelty, dismissiveness, and downright mockery that lives on Twitter (and other social media sites) within the Christian community is breathtaking and disheartening. Being theologically correct does not give you the license to be mean. Defending a biblical truth doesn't make it okay to mock the person you disagree with. Standing for what you are convinced is right does not give you permission to question the thinking and integrity of the person who has taken another position. Theology, properly understood and lived, will never produce meanness, misogyny, disrespect, mockery, or cruelty of any kind, ever. It produces just the opposite.

Listen to the words of Paul, who says that if the truth you say you believe and understand doesn't result in love, then maybe you don't understand it as well as you think you do: "The aim of our charge is love that issues from a pure heart and a good conscience and a sincere faith. Certain persons, by swerving from these, have wandered away into vain discussion, desiring to be teachers of the law, without understanding either what they are saying or the things about which they make confident assertions" (1 Tim. 1:5–7).

What straightforward and convicting words. May we pray for grace to always hold truth and love together, never willing to abandon one for the sake of the other.

4. *The normalization of self-righteous responses.* Humility radically changes the way you respond to the sin, weakness, failure, immaturity, error, or opposition of others. If you admit how wrong you are capable of being, how you too can be thoughtless, how prideful you can be, and how patience is still a struggle for you, then it's much harder to go on the attack. And if you know more, understand more deeply, and have arrived at positions that are more biblically right, you have gotten there only by means of the intervention of divine grace.

Humility makes it hard to be quick to criticize, dismiss, or judge others because you know you're numbered among them. It is easy to judge people with the law that you are convinced you keep. It's easy to quickly react judgmentally to wrong when you are convinced you are almost always right. It's all too easy to see others as weaker and lesser, when they haven't lived up to the standard that defines how I think I am living. It's easy to refuse to listen when I have judged another person as having little to offer to someone like me. Self-righteousness turns the human community into a toxic and dangerous place to be, where outrage and judgment are just around the corner and where honesty is dangerous and opinions come at a cost. A spirit of personal always-rightism will never produce patient, humble, loving responses to others. The truth is that none of us has anything of value that we didn't receive and, if we received it, we should neither boast because we have it nor mistreat the person who seems to be without it (see 1 Cor. 4:7).

5. *The normalization of vengeful responses.* A quick scan of Twitter responses reveals that it is not unusual for responses not just to debate, rebuke, or confront, but to harm. A person who is hurt by a post responds in a way that is calculated to hurt in return, to damage a person's reputation, or even to attempt to end someone's career. Here's what we need to remember: vengeful anger is always the result of some person trying to do God's job. There is only one judge of the heart. There is only one who is able to mete out perfectly holy and just judgment. Consider the powerful and practical words of the apostle Paul, in a passage that seems like it was written for today's reactive culture:

> Repay no one evil for evil, but give thought to do what is honorable in the sight of all. If possible, so far as it depends on you, live peaceably with all. Beloved, never avenge yourselves, but leave it to the wrath of God, for it is written, "Vengeance is mine, I will repay, says the Lord." To the contrary, "if your enemy is hungry, feed him; if he is thirsty, give him something to drink; for by so doing you will heap burning coals on his head." Do not be overcome by evil, but overcome evil with good. (Rom. 12:17–21)

How humbling it is to admit that we still have moments when we are tempted to do what God alone is able to do, that is, to deal out the judgment that we believe another person so much needs. So, the exhortation here is always needed, always timely. Paul's directives are clear and, if they were heeded, would transform our culture of reactivity. Never repay evil for evil, ever. Always overcome evil with good. Leave vengeance to the Lord. When Paul says, "Leave it to the wrath of God," he's saying, "Get out of God's way and let him do what he alone is able to do." Human anger that is weaponized by vengeance and unleashed by self-righteousness never produces anything good. Evil in the face of evil only multiples the evil. Only good in the face of evil will produce a harvest of good things.

6. *The normalization of individualism.* Disrespectful, dismissive, vengeful, mocking, motive-judging, and condemning reactions never produce healthy, loving, vulnerable, honest, reconciled, and unified community where confession, repentance, and forgiveness are encouraged. This is the kind of community God carefully designed for us to live in. By his wise plan, it is not good for us to live alone. We are born with the need for relationships. Each of our lives is a community project. So we must always respond to one another with the humble recognition that we need one another. This means responding in ways that strengthen our community, deepen our bonds, and stimulate candid, loving communication.

The "drive-by-shooting" reactions to something that you disagree with or that has disturbed you in some way is individualism run amok. It's an "I don't need you, here's what I think of you, and I don't care what this does to our relationship" way of responding. If you keep slugging me when I speak, I am going to quit speaking to you. If you are a believer, the life that God has planned for you is entirely relational. That is why Jesus prayed that we would be one as the Trinity is one. This is why Paul says we should do everything we can to preserve the unity of the body of Christ. This is why we are directed to forgive as God has forgiven us. This is why we are called to speak the truth, but to speak it in love. We are not little human islands; no, by God's design we are connected in mutually dependent community. Denial of our foundational relational design allows a culture of reactivity to chip away at our trust in one another and the community of interdependency that is essential for us all.

7. *The normalization of the love of controversy.* It needs to be noted that there is an important difference between the love of theological purity and intellectual integrity and the love of controversy. Our culture of reactivity is a culture on a hunt for controversy. It is propelled by the thrill of the hunt and that scintillating moment when you draw your word weapon, take aim, and pull the verbal trigger. It's enjoying watching how many bullets it takes before the person drops. The love of controversy sadly views other human beings not as your community but as your prey. And what gives you joy is not the messy process of love but the thrill of having captured your quarry again.

A love for truth that doesn't produce a life of love is a love for something else masquerading as a love for truth. Theology that doesn't produce a life of love is bad theology. Holding your insights in a way that produces a lifestyle that loves the fight more than the thing that is worth fighting for keeps you from using truth in the way it was meant to be used. We will all find ourselves in moments of controversy, but it's the love of it that never produces anything good.

8. *The normalization of tribalism.* It is always easier to react to a group that you're not part of. No one holds a sign in a protest that

says "My tribe is the problem." The goal of our communication should not be preserving the power of our tribe but creating an intertribe culture of respect, relationship, mutual dependency, and learning. God works to do in us and through us something that is not natural for us. He works to break down the barriers that separate us from one another. "There is neither Jew nor Greek, there is neither slave nor free, there is no male and female, for you are all one in Christ Jesus" (Gal. 3:28). God is not working to destroy the distinctions of ethnicity and gender, which he created, give him glory, and propel the work he means to do in us, but by grace he is working to transform the way we think about and respond to those distinctions. By the Creator's design, we don't just need people who are like us; we desperately need people who are unlike us. The community that God is working to create is not tribal; it is universal, gathering all the tribes together as one.

Our culture of reactivity is a culture of tribalism. The message we communicate is, "I don't respect you because I don't respect your tribe, so I will respond to you in ways that I would never think of responding to someone in my tribe." This means I live in a tribal culture of groupthink and group do, never benefiting from the challenging and potentially transforming insights from someone from another tribe. We are too divided, separated into racial, political, theological, ethnic, economic, gender, age, and class groups. We build walls not bridges. We yell over the wall at one another, but we don't stop to listen, consider, and learn. We make uninformed assumptions that turn potential helpers into enemies while thinking we know best and, because we do, we don't need "them." We even react against our own when we think they are building bridges and not shoring up our walls. Tribalism produces endless war and leaves lots of casualties but never produces the community that is essential if we are ever going to grow to be what God intended us to be and together live as he created us to live.

*

As I came to the end of this chapter, conviction set in. Conviction is a good thing and should not be resisted. It is God giving eyes to see and opening hearts to receive. Conviction is our heavenly Father drawing us close and keeping us near. It is important for me to confess that the things which I have said we cannot allow to be normalized still tempt me and at times are sadly too natural for me. I am sure you could confess the same. I wish I could say that all of my written and verbal responses to others are patient, loving, respectful, and thoughtful. I wish I could say that I always speak the truth in love. I wish I could say that all of my responses are devoid of harmful anger. I wish I could say that there is never a moment when I'd rather be right than loving. I wish I could say that nothing I have written in this chapter addresses me, but I can't.

I write as a man in need of grace and as one who is thankful that God's grace doesn't just forgive; it empowers. And it doesn't just empower; it transforms. It is the presence and power of this grace that is the hope and foundation of this book. By grace we are not left to our antisocial instincts, to our tribalistic pride, or to the fact that vengeance is often more attractive to us than forgiveness. We are not left to ourselves. The grace God offers us is not a onetime gift. No, he lavishly gives us grace upon grace upon grace. May we together confess that we too are tempted to participate in this culture of reactivity and, as we confess, let us run to the only one who can help us, because he alone has the power to transform the thoughts, desires, motives, and choices of our hearts.

2

Wholesome Talk

IT WAS A BOOK TITLE that said it all: *Vulgarians at the Gate* (Prometheus, 2001). Steve Allen had entertained America on television for decades, but now as an older man he was grieved at the coarsening of the medium he had dedicated much of his life and gifts to. His book is not the comedic ride you would expect from Allen but rather a stinging critique of a medium gone vulgar. *Vulgarians* was published more than twenty years ago; think of what Allen would write about Twitter, Facebook, Instagram, or TikTok today.

Why have these wonderful tools of human communication seemingly been taken over by coarse, angry, vulgar, cruel, vengeful posts from almost every side? Why does a mocking response draw a crowd, quite willing to join in? Why do we seem to be aggressors on the hunt rather than participants in a conversation? Why does controversy magnetize us? Whatever happened to wholesome talk?

Eric Hoffer, the hugely popular street-level American philosopher, commented on the power of malice: "It is remarkable by how much a pinch of malice enhances the penetrating power of an idea

Emotional Warmth

~In the light~

or an opinion. Our ears, it seems, are wonderfully attuned to sneers and evil reports about our fellow men."[1] With these words Hoffer proved to be a better theologian than he probably knew.

Jesus said that as sinners we love darkness rather than light. As long as sin still lives inside of us, there is in us an attraction to evil. It is a humbling thing to admit. The power of sin's temptation is that it appeals to something inside of us. Here is the clearest way to biblically view Hoffer's observation. It is always the evil that is still inside of us that hooks us to the evil that is outside of us. This is why we are attracted to the dark and damaging words of gossip or why we laugh at mockery that should repel us. This is why we are not only attracted to malice but we soon join in, or why we spend way too much screen time tracking down the latest controversy. None of this would happen if it didn't feed something that our hearts desire.

What does this have to do with wholesome talk? Let's go back to Steve Allen's *Vulgarians*. Allen was right, but not at a deep enough level. It's not just that we hear and read words on popular and social media that would have shocked us not too many years ago, and it's not just that vulgar sexual terms and blasphemous use of the Lord's name have become regular; it's what is behind those words that needs both examination and the kind of transformation that only grace can provide. Why do we glory in a put-down, a mocking hot take, or verbal cruelty? We have a problem, but it's deeper than vocabulary.

I want to spend the rest of this chapter examining one passage from Ephesians that exposes why we react toward one another the way we do, what a much better way looks like, and what makes that

1   Eric Hoffer, *The Passionate State of Mind, and Other Apohorisms* (New York: Harper, 1955), 167.

better way possible. This passage sits right in the middle of Paul's lengthy portrait of what it looks like in everyday life and relationships to live in light of the gospel of the grace of Jesus Christ: "Let no corrupting talk come out of your mouths, but only such as is good for building up, as fits the occasion, that it may give grace to those who hear. And do not grieve the Holy Spirit of God, by whom you were sealed for the day of redemption" (Eph. 4:29–30).

The first thing that is vital to notice is that Paul's discussion of wholesome (not corrupting) communication is not a discussion of vocabulary. He doesn't define "corrupting" talk by giving us a list of forbidden words. Now, this doesn't mean that we are free to use sexually explicit, damning, or culturally impolite terms whenever and however we wish. But this passage does warn us that defining unwholesome talk by a list of words is too low of a standard. For Paul, "corrupting talk" is first and foremost a matter of the intention of the heart. You can cruelly mock a person and not use one single bad word. You can post something that is meant to harm while not using certain offensive words. You can react vengefully while priding yourself that you haven't damned the person. If, as the family of God, we are ever going to address the culture of harmful reactivity that lives not just in the surrounding culture but also in our family, we must get below the level of vocabulary and shine the light of biblical wisdom on the thoughts, desires, and intentions of our hearts.

Here's how this passage immediately hits me. It sets for me an impossibly high standard, one that somehow, someway I fall short of every day. I wish I could say that everything I speak or write flows out of the kind of intentionality that this passage calls us to. I wish I could say that I have matured to the point where I never react in a way that resists the beautiful call of these words, but I

for a fellow
my creation
commitment

can't. The seemingly impossible standard of the wholesome talk in Ephesians 4:29 always carries my thoughts to James 3:

> Not many of you should become teachers, my brothers, for you know that we who teach will be judged with greater strictness. For we all stumble in many ways. And if anyone does not stumble in what he says, he is a perfect man, able also to bridle his whole body. If we put bits into the mouths of horses so that they obey us, we guide their whole bodies as well. Look at the ships also: though they are so large and are driven by strong winds, they are guided by a very small rudder wherever the will of the pilot directs. So also the tongue is a small member, yet it boasts of great things. *Shared interest values fastinating*
>
> How great a forest is set ablaze by such a small fire! And the tongue is a fire, a world of unrighteousness. The tongue is set among our members, staining the whole body, setting on fire the entire course of life, and set on fire by hell. For every kind of beast and bird, of reptile and sea creature, can be tamed and has been tamed by mankind, but no human being can tame the tongue. It is a restless evil, full of deadly poison. With it we bless our Lord and Father, and with it we curse people who are made in the likeness of God. From the same mouth come blessing and cursing. My brothers, these things ought not to be so. Does a spring pour forth from the same opening both fresh and salt water? Can a fig tree, my brothers, bear olives, or a grapevine produce figs? Neither can a salt pond yield fresh water. (James 3:1–12)

Allies
family
d n

Open your heart to the strongly stated warning of these words. How does James characterize the problem with our talk (tongues)?

"If anyone does not stumble in what he says, he is a perfect man."

"The tongue is a fire, a world of unrighteousness."

"No human being can tame the tongue."

"It is a restless evil, full of deadly poison."

"With it we bless our Lord and Father, and with it we curse people who are made in the likeness of God."

These are strong, convicting, and disheartening words that alert us to the fact that what we are considering in this book is not a little thing that we should find a way somehow to live with. No, what we are dealing with is something that sets people, relationships, families, government, communities, schools, and the church on fire. So, we have to ask, "How do we tame the untamable?" How do we harness what James says is a "restless evil"? What hope of change do we have for our culture of reactivity? Let the power of the words of James 3 convict you, but don't let them discourage you. Ephesians 4:29–30 has powerful answers for us: "Let no corrupting talk come out of your mouths, but only such as is good for building up, as fits the occasion, that it may give grace to those who hear. And do not grieve the Holy Spirit of God, by whom you were sealed for the day of redemption" (Eph. 4:29–30).

Let me go back to what I earlier observed about Paul's application of the gospel to our speech. He focuses not just on our words but also on our hearts—the intention behind our reactions and responses. This is exactly where the attention needs to be. Jesus said that every word that comes out of our mouth finds its origin and formation in our heart (see Luke 6:43–45). Your reactions will only ever go where your heart has already gone. So, a commitment to wholesome talk isn't first a commitment to a restricted vocabulary but rather to change at the level of the thoughts, desires, intentions,

20% from brain stem
thinking to feeling

now do I know what I think until I hear what I say
80% - © creates afrom cell information to brain

80% feeling level
hart informs

©

and choices of the heart. Paul delineates three heart commitments that will always lie behind a culture of wholesome responses to one another.

Every Response Must Be Shaped by a Consideration of the Person

"Only such as is good for building up." Here is an application of "love your neighbor as yourself" to our world of communication. It is a call to responses that are deeply loving. I am not posting what I am posting because it makes me happy or it satisfies some philosophical, theological, cultural, or tribal desire in me. This is a call to other-centered communication. My reaction is not done for *me* but out of loving consideration for *you*. There is something that I want for you, but it's not that you would be simply proven wrong, put in your place, exposed for what you are, proven to be the fool, exposed as a member of a certain tribe, soundly mocked, getting what belongs to you, knocked off your pedestal, or harmed in some way. No, what this passage calls me to is the polar opposite of what the culture of reactivity does and ultimately produces.

Imagine even stopping to think of the person you're reacting to as *a person*, that is, a being made in the image of God. Imagine taking the time to think of others in their world, having a normal set of responsibilities and people who love them and whom they love. Imagine considering how they have been hit with the burdens, temptations, and heartaches of life in this fallen world. Imagine taking time to think about how they will be impacted by your words.

Now imagine responding not just because you like the verbal skirmish but because, out of love, you really do want the person to benefit from and be built up by whatever it is you are about to

blurt...
languaged ♡

joost blurt

post, tweet, or say. Imagine caring enough to want that person to learn something new, to grow in self-awareness, to have a deeper confidence in God, to be encouraged in some way, or to gain new courage or motivation. What if every reaction were preceded by this kind of other-centered consideration? What if you only ever spoke to build up? How different would your reactions be? How many previous reactions would you have to delete?

"Only such as is good for building up" means that the core character quality of wholesome communication is love. In these words is a call to intentional, focused commitment to loving communication, no matter how wrong you think people are, no matter what you think of their tribe, no matter how hurt or angry they have made you, and no matter how high you think the stakes are. When love is the expendable ingredient in our communication, there is no end to the hurt, chaos, division, and harm our reactions will produce. When you refuse to abandon this call to love and determine to only ever speak the truth in love, you will say what you need to say in a radically different manner and with an entirely different tone. The darkness of social media isn't difficult to understand; it is the darkness of the failure to love. The human community, as God designed it, cannot function without love. Human communication cannot work without love. Without love, human interactivity becomes a war zone with a list of casualties too many to number.

We are not islands. We all need builder-uppers around us. We all need encouragement. We all need loving rebuke. We all need insight. We all need fresh starts and new beginnings. We all need to know that we are not alone. We all need gifts of patience and grace along the way. We all need love, there are no haves and have-nots. Each of us needs to be built up and each of us is

(margin notes, handwritten)
end of Knowledge is action Kindness

do Say

Key · · Change transformation

big hearted
heart felt 37
large heart

choice
→ meditate
→ pray

ok—

called to be a builder. This mutuality of community is a beautiful gift from a wise and loving God. It seems that we have devalued this gift and viewed being right, winning the day, and putting someone in his or her place as being more valuable. The human community will continue to be harmed and our digital meeting places will continue to be dark and dangerous as long as tearing down seems more attractive than building up.

Every Response Must Be Shaped by an Understanding of the Situation

"As fits the occasion." Before you react, consider the moment you're speaking into. First, make sure you carefully read the whole post and pay attention to the comments that follow. If you're in a face-to-face conversation, pay attention to the situation and location of the conversation. I have received many critical and angry comments on Twitter by people who apparently did not read the entire post because if they had, they probably wouldn't have responded as they did. Don't allow yourself to quickly react to a title of an article you have not carefully read.

Second, before you react, reflect on the cultural moment. Is this a moment of cultural confusion? Is it a time of cultural grief? Are the various cultural tribes angry and at battle? Has the culture lost its way? Is it a cultural bandwagon moment that everyone seems to be jumping on? Then ask yourself, "Why do I feel the need to respond? What am I hoping my reaction will accomplish? Do I have anything to add that would clarify, advance, or calm the conversation? Is my desire to react born out of hurt and anger or motivated by loving concern?"

As a believer I should think about what kind of moment this is for the church. Is this a volatile, divisive issue for the body of Christ? How much impact is this having on my everyday Christian community? Are there threats to the gospel? How is the church of Jesus Christ being viewed, both in the way it understands and how it handles the issue? How is the current discussion and the way it is conducted affecting the reputation and ministry of the church? As a member of the body of Christ, how should I interact with the issue at hand? As a believer, why do I feel compelled to join in? Are my reactions needed? Will good result? Ephesians 4 reminds us that wholesome communication flows from a careful consideration of the moment, the situation, and the occasion.

Every Response Must Be Shaped by the Goal of Grace

"That it may give grace to those who hear." Chapter 4 of this book explores what it means to have your words rooted in grace, so I will be brief here. Every reaction must be shaped by a commitment to the right process of communication, and the right process is shaped by what you want your words to achieve. Paul says everything you say, no matter when you say it, no matter who you say it to, and no matter what the topic is, must have grace as its goal.

Whenever I talk about responding with grace as a goal, I am met with misunderstanding. When people hear the word *grace*, they think I mean being nice, being permissive, being passive, or choosing not to deal with difficult things. It is important to recognize that God's grace is anything but passive. Grace never calls wrong right. If wrong were right, there would be no need for the rescuing, intervening, and transformative operation of grace. Grace is not about ignoring wrong; it is a radically different way of dealing with wrong. Responding in grace requires humbly admitting your inability, coupled with a robust trust in the power of God.

*

So what exactly does Ephesians 4:29 mean for the world of communication, both personal and digital? The answer is found in James 1:19–20: "Know this, my beloved brothers: let every person be quick to hear, slow to speak, and slow to anger; for the anger of man does not produce the righteousness of God." There is so much instruction about gospel living and communication packed into this verse, which I will cover in later chapters, but here I want to focus on the three phrases "quick to hear, slow to speak, and slow to anger." It's as if Ephesians 4:29 were written as an explanation of what it looks like to be committed to listen first, allow time before you speak, and never speak out of anger. If we all were committed to having these three directives shape our reactions to one another, Twitter, Facebook, Instagram, and many of our personal relationships would be immediately transformed. The toxic dump of cruel, mocking, disrespectful, dismissive, and vengeful communication would be gone, the power of tribalism would be weakened, and the wisdom that is only ever attained collectively would have room to grow.

But here's the rub. For this to happen, we all need to be visited by rescuing and empowering grace. Talk toxicity is a heart problem that is solved only by redeeming grace. I must confess, I do like to talk more than I like to listen. I do have moments when I let anger shape my words. Here's the humbling thing we all need to confess: toxic talk is never caused by the one you're talking to. It's always caused by you. Likewise, wholesome talk is never initiated

40

by the one you're talking to. It always starts with you. Like every other spiritual need, God meets our reactivity trouble with forgiving, rescuing, and transforming grace.

We have a problem. It's harming us, our unity, our ability to grow together, and our witness. But there is help for the taking in the powerful grace of Jesus.

When I
Because

When you
I Feel

When I
I Feel

3

Sin

MY YOUNG FRIEND SAT DOWN for dinner, and I knew right away that he was discouraged. I asked him how he was doing, and his answer was to hand me his cell phone. It was opened to an email he had received that morning. He is one of the young pastors I meet with. I love these times and these men. I listen to their ministry horror stories and try to comfort them with the gospel and give them insight on how to respond to the kinds of things every pastor faces. But over the last couple years, I've begun to understand that something very different is going on. Pastors are under attack in a way they have never been before. No, I am not talking about the attacks that you would expect from a godless culture. I'm talking about attacks from the very people that they have sought to love and serve. Yes, pastors blow it at times and, yes, there are users who find their way into ministry who should never be there and who leave a trail of damage behind them. I know people who have endured the harm of church hurt. But I am meeting with good and godly men who, although they are imperfect and still maturing, love God and love their people and have dedicated their lives to the soul care of gospel-centered pastoral ministry.

I took his phone in my hands and began to read. What a message to receive Monday morning following a long and demanding Sunday of public and private ministry. His medium-sized Midwest church had once been a joyful place to serve. It was an imperfect and messy community, but it was a community of love nonetheless. He and his wife had moved from the East, had settled in to a productive life of ministry, and had been there for ten years. He never imagined that he would want to leave this church or that he would someday daydream about leaving pastoral ministry altogether. The words I read were not loving, thankful, or even respectful. They were written in anger and filled with judgments of character and motive. The husband and wife, who wrote the email together, said they could not continue to have my friend as their pastor, and they were immediately canceling their membership. They didn't ask for an appointment to talk and share their concerns. The email was not an invitation to talk; no, it was an accusatory bomb drop. It was an email version of a drive-by shooting, but by people with whom he shared life, love, and ministry. It wasn't his first, and it wouldn't be the last.

It wasn't his theology, his preaching, his pastoral care, or even his personality that they had come to hate. It was his perceived politics. Nothing about his preaching was political, in the true sense of what the word means. He preached gospel-infused messages, walking through one portion of God's word after another. They thought he had forsaken the faith because he preached the Bible's justice themes when they were in the text he was expounding. From their perspective, he didn't seem to be as politically conservative as they thought a true Christian should be. So, in a Sunday-night reaction to something he had said that morning that angered them, they fired off their termination email. He woke up to the bomb drop from people he loved, tried not to waste the whole morning wallowing in the toxicity, and then came to have lunch with me. This was not the first of these situations I witnessed, and I'm sure it won't be the last.

We have drifted far from a lifestyle of wholesome talk, one in which you can expect others to listen well, take time to consider, and speak with understanding, respect, and grace. So we are going to spend the next five chapters examining the biblical worldview that lies underneath the call to wholesome communication, whether face-to-face or screen-to-screen. These chapters will explore five biblical themes that are the root perspectives of how the apostle Paul, in Ephesians 4, understood we should communicate. I deeply believe that these biblical themes, taken seriously, are the death of any culture of reactive toxicity. The five themes are *sin*, *grace*, *identity*, *glory*, and *eternity*. Each has the power to expose us, convict us, restore us, and transform us.

✳

Saying that our damage-producing culture of reactivity is a sin problem is obvious, but it is nonetheless important to say. But we must also look at what a deeply humbling and insight-giving perspective this is. When you are willing to say that there is such a thing as sin, you have opened the door to the deepest, most practical understanding of human dysfunction that you could ever consider. The Bible elaborately unpacks, from cover to cover, what sin is and what sin does. This unpacking begins with the first historical account after the account of creation. In fact, it is not an overstatement to say that all we need to do is carefully examine the sad biblical stories of Genesis 3 and 4 to see in living color what sin is and what sin does.

Sin Is Self-Centered

God had lovingly designed Adam and Eve, gifted them with one another, placed them in a beautiful garden where they would find everything they needed, set protective boundaries for them, and blessed them with his presence and love. It truly was a life in paradise. It is this context that makes the self-centeredness of Adam and Eve so shocking and clear. Why did they step outside of God's boundaries and eat what was forbidden? The answer is *self-centeredness*. It wasn't hunger that motivated them; no, their motivations are exposed in the narrative that has been retained for us. They ate because they thought they would be like God and because the fruit would deliver wisdom to them. Take note that they didn't need wisdom. They were in relationship with the ultimate source of all wisdom. What attracted them was independent wisdom, that is, wisdom that wasn't connected to submission to God. They desired the autonomous, self-sufficient existence that only God has. They wanted to be in the center of their world, free to think and live as they wanted. In that horrible self-centered, self-glorying moment they stepped outside of God's loving boundaries and paradise was no more.

In its essence, sin is about living for yourself. Sin is driven by what we want, when we want it, how we want it, and where we want it, no matter what. It is driven by no greater value than my wants, my needs, and my feelings. Sin is by its very nature anti-authority and antisocial. At its core, sin doesn't care who is in charge and how others are affected. Sin shrinks the field of my concern down to my own desires. It's me in the center, it's me in control, and it's me writing my own rules.

The culture of toxic reactivity is a culture of self-centeredness. It's not driven by love for others. It's not propelled by love for truth. It rebels against higher authority. It doesn't display a commitment to ongoing community and communication. Toxic reactivity says I have a right to my opinion and I have a right to express it however I wish. I have a right to call you out, to put you down, and to dismiss your tribe, no matter what the consequences. I don't care who you are, what you have achieved, or what your present situation is. I will fire away behind my screen however I wish, and no one will take away my right to do so. Reactivity is speakers or writers assuming a godlike position, responding as they wish. Their only allegiance is to themselves. It is in the soil of this self-centeredness that disrespect, mockery, misogyny, cruelty, vengeance, and dismissal grow.

Where the self-centeredness of sin lives and grows, true, productive, insight-producing, relationship-building, unity-producing, change-motivating communication dies. When we react, we're not offering one another nutrients by which we may grow; we are shooting verbal bullets at one another that injure us and kill any hope we may have that we can launch our thoughts into an environment of thoughtful consideration.

It's not hard to get at the root of our reactivity problem. The question is, Will we humbly confess the self-centeredness of sin that still seduces us all and takes our talk where our Creator never intended it to go?

Sin Rebels against Authority

It is important to recognize that Adam and Eve's choice to eat the forbidden fruit was not a breaking of some abstract rule. No, what they did was a direct rebellion against the authority of God. Their disobedience was vertical and personal. They were walking away from a life of submission to the authority of God and setting themselves up as their own authority. Human life, properly lived, is always shaped by a willing submission to God's authority and the human authorities he has set up to represent him. Healthy, productive human communication is the result of a submission to a higher authority than your own. Good communication always submits to a set of rules that you didn't make. Good communication, which never harms and always produces a harvest of good fruit, submits itself to love God above all else and your neighbor as yourself.

The culture of toxic reactivity submits to no authority but the authority of self. It recognizes no rules of communication other than the rules the speaker or writer sets for him or herself. Reactivity takes no time to consider communication rights and wrongs. The culture of reactivity doesn't wait to think of the greater good. It doesn't take the time necessary to communicate in a way that is free from harm in any way. The culture of reactivity is more motivated by the attention-getting hot take than it is by genuine love for the receiver. It's a culture that glories in the takedown rather than in patience, forgiveness, and love. Reactivity has a loud, aggressive voice, rather than a kind, measured, thoughtful, and thought-provoking response. It's driven by the right to speak rather than a consideration about how best to speak. Like Adam and Eve, toxic reactivity at its core rejects God's authority and the essentiality of the loving community that he created for healthy human functioning. The question is, Will we sit behind our screens as our own authority and use our words as we wish for purposes no greater than our own?

Sin Is Independent

We were not designed by our wise and loving Creator to live alone. We were made to live in a vibrant vertical and horizontal community. Fellowship with God and with others is an essential ingredient in our spiritual health and proper living. Independence is a seductive delusion that never takes us anywhere good. Look where the quest for independence took Adam and Eve. The religion of the Old and New Testaments is foundationally and practically relational. God, who himself is a community, crafted those made in his image to live in community with him and one another. Healthy, mutually loving, and mutually serving relationships are not a human luxury—they are a human necessity. To be human is to be a social being. This means that isolated, self-sufficient, and independent living is not just a denial of my spirituality; it is also a denial of my humanity.

This is why the antisocial behavior on social media is so harmful and alarming. The powerfully influential culture found online denies the Creator's design and, because it does, cannot ultimately work. It cannot be constructive. It will be destructive. It is a denial of the mutual love and mutual dependency that is the soil in which healthy living grows. Hateful takedowns are never posted by someone who is committed to ongoing relationship and healthy mutual edification. This reactive culture puts a higher value in securing a hit than it does on the person taking the hit. A hunt for the next good shot is never where "love your neighbor as yourself" will take you. The person finding joy in taking down another person has about as much commitment to loving relationships as the hunter has to the duck he is hunting. This is a sad deconstructing of life as the Creator designed it to be: me in relationship to you, together in relationship to God. A community.

Sin devalues relationships for the glory of self. Sin always ends up harming our relationships in some way. Look what sin did to Adam and Eve's relationship. Consider the horrible fruit of sin in the relationship of their sons, Cain and Abel. Imagine I am angry at you because of something you said and in my anger I get up so close to you that you can feel my breath, while I say inflammatory, accusatory, and hurtful things about you. What are you thinking at that moment? I doubt you're thinking, "Paul loves me so much. This is so helpful. I am learning so much. I wish he would do this more." No, you are crushed, and all you want to do is get away and out from under the onslaught. As I'm up in your face, I'm not forming a relationship with you; I am harming whatever relationship we have. You are not listening to me. You are not learning from me. You are not feeling grateful for me. You are not hoping to engage me further. Nothing constructive results. Neither person is better because of the encounter. Why would we think getting up in a person's face via a screen and a social media post would have a different result?

If the aim of the religion of Christianity is love out of a pure heart, then much of the Christianity on social media is false religion. It may be theologically knowledgeable and biblically literate, but it is the religion of the Pharisees. It is a culture of pride, self-righteousness, and legalism. It binds burdens on people rather than helping them bear their burdens. It is accusatory and condemning rather than loving and forgiving. It mocks those considered less righteous or not as theologically informed. It hunts for reasons to judge and finds joy in disrespectful, cruel attacks. It lacks the kind words of a tender heart. It professes a love for truth but is really driven by a love of self. It is obsessed with its own voice, while seldom listening very well.

A Christian media culture that does not regularly exhibit the fruit of the spirit is actually Pharisaism, that is, the kingdom of self masquerading as the kingdom of God. On his way to the cross, the strongest words Jesus spoke were to those who promoted such a culture (see Matt. 23). Humbling, rescuing, forgiving, and transforming grace doesn't produce independent, relationship-harming, proud, disrespectful toxicity. It produces the opposite.

I don't think I am particularly naive, but I am regularly shocked by the manner at which "Christians" talk to one another online. I am regularly dismayed at the disrespectful reactions to spiritual leaders. I am not saying we should never post questions to our leaders or engage them in a respectful conversation or even debate with them. But when I read, "Dude, just quit tweeting," or "Bro, just shut up," or "_____ just get back in the kitchen and bake something," or "You can be in ministry and still be stupid," I get heartsick for the church of Jesus Christ and for the state of its culture. We were made to live in loving community with one another where we grow to know God and his truth in union with one another. Anything that harms this community harms us, stunts our growth, and moves us away from the life Jesus died to make possible for us.

As I was thinking of the current independent, relationship-devaluing Christian social media culture, I thought of the words of Paul at the end of Ephesians 3. This statement is the capstone of his discussion of the theology of the grace of Jesus Christ: "That you, being rooted and grounded in love, may have strength to comprehend *with all the saints* what is the breadth and length and height and depth, and to know the love of Christ that surpasses knowledge, that you may be filled with all the fullness of God" (Eph. 3:17–19). Paul is saying that the hermeneutic of the gospel is a community project. We will fully comprehend the redeeming magnitude of the love of God only when we are developing our understanding in community with other believers. Gospel theology is never developed independently. Practical, transformational gospel understanding is a community project. The gospel is only ever fully known in the context of humble, approachable, and mutually dependent relationships with other believers. Any behavior that harms those relationships harms our potential for fully understanding truths that so desperately need to be known.

Charismatic believers need conversation with Reformed believers and vice versa. Baptist and Presbyterian believers need to be able to talk respectfully and listen humbly to one another. Politically conservative believers need to talk with those who are not so conservative. Leaders need to be in conversation with those who are not leaders. Young and old believers need to be able to communicate with one another. White believers and Black believers need to be in gospel conversation with one another. Our communication needs to cross racial, ethnic, political, age, gender, and doctrinal lines. We are not a collection of individuals. We are not an assemblage of tribes, but rather we are one in Christ. Any reaction that does not value the unity of this community harms the very thing that is essential for the gospel to be understood by our minds, embraced by our hearts, and bear fruit in our lives. Toxic reactivity is the enemy of true Christianity because it damages the community that true Christianity holds dear.

Repudiation of proud, independent, and antisocial Christianity that loves winning more than loving must begin with a willingness in each of us to confess and repent of instances when we have taken part in this culture that has moved so far from what God has designed. There is a better way, and grace makes it possible.

Sin Is Vengeful

Having differences is one thing, but hating and wanting to harm the other side is another thing altogether. The seeds of vengeance developed very soon after sin entered the world in the garden of Eden. It began with Adam and Eve pointing the finger of blame. Sin makes it much easier to point out the sin, weakness, failure, inadequacy, hypocrisy, logical fallacy, immaturity, and bias of others than to recognize and confess our own. Sin causes us to think of ourselves as way more righteous than we actually are and others as way more unrighteous than they actually are. We will take a microscope to examine every minute detail of the writings of someone outside of our tribe while seldom giving the same attention to the writings of those we agree with. We are all too quick to assign blame. We are too quick to question the character and motives behind the words on the page. It is all very self-righteous and destructive to the community, conversation, mission, and reputation of the people of God.

But the passive vengeance of blame often morphs into the more active vengeance of harm. We see this in Genesis 4 in a horrible act of sibling homicide. But we also see it on social media in ways that don't always seem so horrible. Some posts are an invitation to a conversation, some are a challenge to a debate, some question the validity of a point made or the qualifications of the person posting; but then there are those that are intended to harm a person's reputation or to silence her voice or to get her audience to join in canceling her. It is an attempt to do what God alone is wise and holy enough to do (see Rom. 12:17–21). I have found the warnings of Leviticus 19:17–18 both sobering and helpful: "You shall not hate your brother in your heart, but you shall reason frankly with your neighbor, lest you incur sin because of him. You shall not take vengeance or bear a grudge against the sons of your own people, but you shall love your neighbor as yourself: I am the Lord." Holding a grudge against someone, failing to be reasonable in your response, and engaging in vengeful reactions are all the fruit of hatred in your heart. This is a hard pill to swallow, but I would ask you to humbly open your heart. Could it be that the power and character of your reactions on social media are not driven by your love for truth or your desire to expose what is wrong but are instead driven by hatred in your heart? A hate-producing grudge against a person or his tribe will never produce reasonableness in your response. No, it will always cause you to sin against your neighbor, passively or actively. Loving your neighbor as yourself will never produce disrespectful mockery, slams against a person's character, straw man accusations, or any other form of verbal cruelty. If we use the lens of Leviticus 19:17–18, we have to admit that underneath our public Christianity there appears to be a whole lot of private hatred.

We don't have just a truth problem; we have a massive love problem that is played out every day on the communication platforms we all use. Love reads and listens carefully and assigns the best intention to the writer's or speaker's words. Hate speaks loudly while not reading or listening well and assigns the worst intentions to the writer's words. Sin turns those who were designed to live in communities of love into haters who damage the health of the very communities that are a vital part of the Creator's commitment to their welfare and thriving. When you feel compelled to react, what is the heart behind that compulsion?

Sin Is a Problem We All Have

This may seem obvious, but on this side of eternity sin is still a problem all of us have. Yes, the power of sin has been broken in the life, death, and resurrection of Jesus, but the presence of sin still remains. We will experience the final death of sin, but we are not there yet. So we are all susceptible to sin's seduction. We are capable of carrying hatred in our hearts, we are capable of loving vengeance more than mercy, we are capable of shocking self-glory and self-righteousness, and we are capable of being more eager to blame than confess. So we all stand in need of the grace of rescue, not first from one another but from ourselves. We need to pray with David for a clean heart and a right spirit (see Ps. 51). And we need to live with the confidence that when we cry out for help, God willingly hears and answers, greeting us with grace that is more than up to the task. His grace guarantees a future when we will be free of this toxicity, but it also guarantees fresh starts and new beginnings right here, right now.

4

Grace

YEARS AGO I EXPERIENCED a moment of tender, life-changing grace. It changed me and the trajectory of my life. With a thankful heart, I have relived that moment again and again, wondering what I would be, where I would be, and what I would be doing without this moment of gracious interruption. I was proud and immature, and I had done many things wrong, but the onslaught of criticism and the questions of my character and qualifications had left me beaten, bruised, discouraged, and defensive. All I wanted to do was run, and I had made concrete plans to do so. But a bountifully loving God sent a tender loving man to interrupt my depressing private conversation with words of grace. I was in the wrong; words of rebuke would have been appropriate, but they would not have rescued me. I would have received them as just another verbal beating. What melted my heart and changed my life was grace, poured out in patient words of forgiveness and love.

I was confronted that day by a truth I have given my life to write and speak about: that *God makes his invisible grace visible by sending people of grace to give grace to people who need grace.* Grace is the most powerful force of transformation in the universe. It has the power to turn liars into truth tellers. It can turn the proud into the humble. It transforms heretics into biblical scholars. It makes selfish people loving and materialistic people generous. It turns rebellious men and women into those who willingly and faithfully obey. It gives sight to blind eyes and causes spiritually deaf people to hear. It reconciles shattered relationships and puts love where hatred once was. It alone has the power to make spiritually dead people to live again. It causes glory-obsessed people to live for the glory of another. It makes comfort-focused people willing to live sacrificially. It puts courage where fear once was, hope where despair lived, and peace where war once raged. It turns idolatry into worship, defeating in the heart what nothing else could ever defeat. The incalculable transforming power of grace should never be minimized or doubted.

As I scan my Twitter feed each day, I wonder if we have functionally lost confidence in the grace that stills lives at the very center of our theology. It seems as though we are placing our hope in another set of tools. If you are trying to fix something in your home and after some effort you drop the tool you are using and pick up another tool, you are doing so because you don't think the tool you have been using is capable of getting the job done. The social media landscape is often seriously lacking in grace. It causes me to think often about the words of 2 Corinthians 10, where the apostle Paul explains that the weapons we fight with are not the weapons of the world. But on social media, we are fighting with the weapons of the world. Although the topics may differ, often the toxic reactivity of Christian social media does not look much different from its secular counterpart. Perhaps our willingness to use the world's weapons reveals a functional lack of confidence in the rescuing and change-producing power of God's grace. In life we all tend to pick up the tool that we think will get the job done.

It should get our attention that the Bible doesn't tell us that the anger of God is what leads people to repentance. For all the gargantuan ferocity of the righteous anger of God against sin, it is his goodness that causes us to listen, to hear, to believe, to confess, and to repent (Rom. 2:4). Mercy triumphs over judgment. When it comes to the way we disagree with one another, debate issues, and respond to concerns, I wonder if we have forgotten the very theology we think we are defending. When you abandon a functional belief in the power of transforming grace, you give room for the toxicity of sin, which still resides in your heart, to shape your reactions to others; cruelty replaces kindness, harshness replaces gentleness, mockery replaces respect, vengeance replaces mercy, hate replaces love, dismissal replaces forgiveness, war-making replaces peacemaking, tribalism replaces a commitment to unity, defensiveness replaces humble approachability, and functional hatred replaces patient love.

This chapter is a call to recommit ourselves to a lifestyle of grace, no matter when, no matter where, no matter about what, and no matter who. Grace is more than a means of attaining a relationship with God and a promise of an eternity with him. Grace is also a welcome to a brand-new way of living. Grace welcomes us to humbly admit our limits and to humbly answer God's call. The theology of grace that splashes across the pages of Scripture is deeply humbling. It requires me to admit that I am not capable of the deepest, most necessary kind of change, that I am a person in need of divine rescue. It also requires me to admit that I have independent power to change no one. If I had the power to fundamentally change another person by the force of my anger, by the power of my logic, or by guilt, shame, or fear, then the life, death, and resurrection of Jesus would not have been necessary. Change at the level of the human heart is always an act of God's grace.

Yes, God uses instruments. That's why we believe in the proclamation of the gospel, in biblical discipleship, in confronting error, in defending biblical truth, in honest discussion and debate, and in teaching, preaching, and counseling. But the vital question we must always ask is, "What is God doing in this moment and how can I be part of it?" It's not about what has made me angry, what I think of the other person, what I want from this moment, what I think of this other tribe, or how I want to be viewed. I am never on center stage; God is. My will is never paramount; God's will is. My hopes and dreams are never the controlling factor; God's plan, purpose, and call are. A culture of grace is about recognizing that God is working out his plan, doing what I could never do, right here, right now, and calling me to be part of it. The theology of God's grace always gives me a higher, grander purpose for my responses than I would otherwise have. Submitting my words to that higher purpose frees me from the reactive toxicity that is so personally and communally destructive.

God's Way of Grace

The Bible is replete with calls for us to commit ourselves to a lifestyle of grace: "Forgive as God has forgiven you"; "Love one another, as I have loved you"; "Be merciful, even as your Father is merciful" (see Eph. 4:32; John 13:34; Luke 6:36). So, it is important to consider what this lifestyle of grace looks like and how it will shape the way we react and respond to one another. There is no better place to go for a description of a lifestyle of grace than Galatians 5. Paul contrasts this lifestyle, which is made possible only by the heart-transforming grace of the Holy Spirit, with the destructive toxicity of sin. "Now the works of the flesh are evident: sexual immorality, impurity, sensuality, idolatry, sorcery, enmity, strife, jealousy, fits of anger, rivalries, dissensions, divisions, envy, drunkenness, orgies, and things like these" (Gal. 5:19–21). Paul puts enmity, strife, jealousy, fits of anger, rivalries, dissensions, and envy right up there with sexual immorality and sorcery as unfruitful works of darkness. It should be sobering to us that while we decry the sexual immorality of the surrounding culture, we have permitted into our Christian social media culture many of the things that the Bible names as the "works of the flesh." These things, according to Paul, are an alien culture to the culture of the kingdom of God. So they have no place in shaping the way we react to one another, no matter what the issue is or to whom we are responding.

Then in the verses that follow, God's way of grace is laid out for us: "But the fruit of the Spirit is love, joy, peace, patience, kindness, goodness, faithfulness, gentleness, self-control" (Gal. 5: 22–23). I call this list "God's way of grace" because these character qualities are made possible only by divine grace. I have no ability whatsoever to turn myself into the kind of person described by this list. This is why we often refer to this list of character qualities as the "fruit of the Spirit."

But these character qualities are also God's means of extending his grace to others through me. Imagine if everything, from our social media reactivity to our personal responses to others, was shaped by this beautiful culture of grace. Imagine every post shaped by love. Imagine each reaction done in a commitment to peace. Imagine always responding in kindness. Imagine every interaction formed out of a gentle and self-controlled heart. Imagine patience keeping you from reacting too quickly. Imagine committing yourself

Words build up?

to words that build up what is good. Imagine being so committed to a lifestyle of grace that nothing and no one could yank you out of it. These are beautiful character traits, and they hold out for us the hope that Christian social media and the Christian presence in society can become beautiful again. No, I don't mean compromising or weak, but beautiful in spirit and manner. If we commit ourselves to the Spirit's work of ongoing transformation, making his purpose our purpose, gone would be the vengeful response, the mocking reaction, the character assassination, the disrespect, the dismissal, the cruelty, and the toxic tribalism that has made social media such a dark place.

At its core the culture of grace is a Christlike culture. When the Bible calls you to Christlikeness, it doesn't then talk about Christ flipping the tables in the temple. It doesn't call you to take out a whip. No, it calls you to take up a cross and die to yourself. If your responses are in more of the flipping tables category, I am afraid you have misunderstood the ongoing plot of God's grace and your part in it. I am deeply moved by John's introduction of Jesus in the first chapter of his Gospel, but I am comforted and convicted by these words particularly: "And the Word became flesh and dwelt among us, and we have seen his glory, glory as of the only Son from the Father, full of grace and truth" (John 1:14). The last five words of this description of the incarnate Son of God should stop us, resound in our minds, and ring in our hearts: "full of grace and truth." Jesus sits at the core of the gospel we hold dear. He is the one we have been called by grace to emulate. He is the one who must sit as Lord in our hearts. Submission to Jesus should shape everything we do and say. The unparalleled power and beauty of Christianity in a sin-darkened world is captured by these five words. If we are serious about following Jesus, they are the banner that we carry, they are our message, and they shape our character. It is important to note that Jesus wasn't just full of truth. If that were all that filled him, we would have no hope. There would be no redemption, no rescue, no forgiveness, and no fresh starts and new beginnings. There would only be a standard too high for us and judgment too holy for us to sustain.

John presents Jesus as being filled not just with truth but also with grace. It is the combination of truth and grace that is our hope in this life and the one to come. If the Messiah would compromise his truth for grace, there would be no hope of satisfying God's righteous requirements. If he would compromise his grace for truth, there would be no tenderhearted sacrifice for sin. In a consistent gospel worldview, truth and grace are never pulled apart, one is never valued more than the other, and neither is ever abandoned. If you speak truth in ways that are devoid of grace, you have, in fact, done violence to the "truth" that you think you are speaking. If you handle grace in a way that compromises truth, the "grace" that you are offering is not really grace at all.

If you commit yourself to being Christlike, you cannot use truth to shame, mock, dismiss, self-righteously judge, or disrespect others. Truth used to harm ceases to be the truth because it gets bent and twisted by other emotions and agendas. Yes, we are called to love and defend truth, but never in ways that are devoid of grace. Many of the reactions I read on social media are devoid of grace. Again and again, it is my assessment that truth, in its gorgeous, life-giving purity, is lost in the toxicity. What comes across isn't deeply wise, illuminating, liberating, correcting, and life-giving. I compare it to trying to build the intricate mechanism of a fine watch with a hammer. What needs to be built is destroyed because the wrong tool is used. If you see a wrecking ball in front of a house in need of repair, you know that house is not being restored; it has been condemned and is about to be torn down. Wrecking-ball responses to the sin, weakness, immaturity, inadequacy, failure, and wrongs of others never build. When we are being Christlike, we will never use truth in ways that harm. Yes, there are strongholds of falsehood that need to be torn down, but always with the commitment to build a beautiful edifice of truth in its place. Sledgehammers that tear down may be exhilarating to use, but you would never want to live in a home that was built only with a sledgehammer.

It takes grace to invest the patience necessary to fully understand your opponent. It takes grace to answer him with calm wisdom. It takes grace to respond lovingly to personal attack. It takes grace to work so that your emotions and your biases don't get in the way. It takes grace to be humbly approachable. It takes grace to speak the truth in love. It takes grace not to compromise Christian community in the name of truth. It takes grace to trust God to do what you are unable to accomplish in the life of another person. It takes grace to hold truth with humility and love. Godly reactions are always infused with grace.

Now, it's important that we not misunderstand what responding in grace means. Here are some helpful points to consider.

Grace never calls wrong right. Grace is a way of responding to wrong. I often talk about the need to have our responses always seasoned with grace. But many people think I am talking about being nice, passive, or just letting things go. Grace never ignores wrong. Grace never calls wrong right. Grace is never passive in the face of evil. If wrong were right, there would be no need for grace. God's recognition of and hatred for sin demands that sin be dealt with, but his grace demands that it be dealt with by mercy and not judgment. Grace always moves toward others with the desire to respond in ways that are redemptive. Grace is loving, hopeful, patient, and forgiving. It is this spirit that shapes the way grace responds to wrong.

Grace replaces condemnation with community. Jesus came not to condemn us but to provide what was necessary so that we could live in vibrant community with him and one another. By his life, death, and resurrection we are reconciled to God, and that reconciliation then enables us to be reconciled to one another. At the end of his life Jesus prayed that we would be one as he is one with the Father. God, who is a community, gave us his grace so we could dwell in such a rich community with one another that it would be comparable only to him. Ephesians 4 calls us to do everything we can to preserve the unity of that community. Whether on social media with a stranger or in a more personal interaction, our words must always be shaped by this community commitment. We must never react in ways that divide, damage, weaken, or destroy the community that Jesus suffered and died for us to enjoy. And we must recognize that God's wise plan for our individual spiritual health is and will always be a community project.

Grace is humble. It is grace that keeps you from being impressed by your own insight. It keeps you from being proud of the size of your platform. It frees you from taking credit for what you could have never produced on your own. It enables you to be able to listen to those who have not achieved what you have. It means you don't speak with the entitlement of a king but with the humility of a servant. Grace keeps you from a self-aggrandizing way of communicating. It keeps you from judging others as lesser and treating them as if they were. It keeps you from using truth to prove to others how smart you are.

Grace is shaped by sympathy and understanding. Hebrews 4:14–16 presents Jesus as a sympathetic and understanding high priest who is touched by the feelings of our infirmities and, because he is, we can turn to him in our time of need with confidence, knowing that he will respond with mercy that is form-fit for the moment. Grace is never cold and unfeeling. Grace never treats issues as being more important than people. Grace is caring, nurturing, and understanding. Think of the social media culture for a moment and consider how lacking it is in sympathy. Post after post essentially says, "I don't care who you are, what you are going through, or how my words will affect you. I will react as I want to react regardless." In a commitment to Christlikeness, Christian social media should be a beacon of sympathetic and understanding communication, that is, the kind of communication that actually communicates in a way that stimulates further communication.

Grace is patient and kind. The history of Scripture is a history of the patience and kindness of the Lord. Through every chapter of the biblical story we watch the mercy of the Lord poured out as he holds back his judgment. You cannot walk through the biblical story without being blown away by God's kindness. He pours blessings down on both believers and rebels. Every day his grace restrains sin, making life livable not just for those who follow him by faith but for everyone. God is the definition of what is good, kind, patient, and loving because he is a God of grace. We are in desperate need of a culture of patience and kindness. We are too quick to react, and we are too comfortable with reacting in ways that fall short of any definition of kindness.

Grace willingly suffers for the sake of another. To commit yourself to be a tool of God's grace as you react and respond to others (which, remember, is God's standard for wholesome communication) is to be willing to suffer. I have had terrible things written about me on social media. I have had people who appreciated my ministry walk away because of what others have said about me, and videos have been made to mock me. My message and my words are often twisted for someone else's agenda. Though these attacks can be hard to take, I have determined not to slug back but to commit myself to my heavenly Father, who judges all things justly. I don't want my use of this powerful tool (social media) to be a war zone, but rather a place where people know they can find loving gospel insight and encouragement. The landscape of social media would be radically different if more people were willing to suffer, not jumping into the fight but responding with soft words formed by a heart of grace.

It takes grace to give grace. Where does God's call to every believer to be a tool of grace in the hands of a God of grace leave us? Well, it leaves me crying out for grace. Being quick to give grace is not natural for me. It's natural for me to be impatient. It's natural for me to be argumentative. It's natural for me to say what I want to say because I want to say it, not because I have considered whom I'm talking to and what it is that they need. It's natural for me to hold on to hurts and let them shape my reactions down the road. It's natural for me to treat members of my tribe differently than those of another tribe. It's natural for me to be more concerned about the sins, weaknesses, failures, inadequacies, biases, hypocrisies, and fallacies of others than I am about my own. So, if I am ever going to react on social media or in personal conversations with grace, I need grace. I need the intervention of God's grace to free me from what is natural for me and empower me to live in the way that God, who knows what is best, has called me to live.

Because of the life, death, and resurrection of Jesus, and because of the presence of the Holy Spirit living within me, this grace is mine for the taking. What good news! I invite you to confess that being a tool of God's grace is unnatural for you, too, and reach out for the grace your Lord so willingly and generously gives.

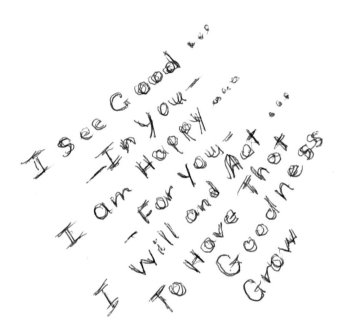

5

Identity

A MAN STOOD OUTSIDE the main entrance to the largest food market in Philadelphia, begging for money. His story was that he was driving with his family over the Ben Franklin Bridge, which spans the Delaware River between Philadelphia and Camden, New Jersey, and his car died. He wanted money to get his family home on public transportation, and then he would decide what to do with his car. You couldn't help but feel sorry for this poor father, caught in a situation that none of us would want to be in. The only problem was that he was there day after day, telling the exact same story. After more than a year of seeing and hearing him, I thought to myself, "Why doesn't he change his location or come up with another story?" My only conclusion was that he was there day after day because it worked. I don't know what this poor man had suffered or why he would ask for money day after day at the door of the market. What I do know is that this man had constructed a false identity. He wasn't a father fearing for the safety of his family, his family wasn't stuck on that bridge and, whatever he wanted money for, it wasn't to get his family home safely. The story he told wasn't who he was and wasn't what his life was about. It was very compelling, it got a lot of attention, and it clearly produced results, but it simply was not true.

I am afraid that social media has become the man outside the market of twenty-first-century life. It is a scary garden of false identity that makes you think things about yourself and others that are not true and, because it does, it has the potential to do way more harm than it does good. There are few more significant, decision-controlling, and life-shaping human thought processes than assigning to yourself some kind of identity. From the earliest days of a child's life to the final days before death, identity is one of the ways we make sense out of life. Whether you know it or not, in the constant private conversation you have with yourself, you are always talking to yourself about who you are. Sometimes it will be a moment of self-rebuke: "You're a grown woman, you should know better." Sometimes it will be for the purpose of courage and motivation: "You trained for this. You can do it." Sometimes it will be to stimulate your faith: "You're a child of God; you are not alone."

The one who created our rationality knows how important identity is to our sanity and proper functioning, so his word has much to say about it. In fact, identity is one of those gospel cords that winds its way through the Bible from Genesis to Revelation. The Bible is clear: who you believe you are will determine how you live. This is why you cannot take a serious look at the toxic reactivity that now shapes so much of our moment-by-moment, day-after-day communication without looking at the topic of identity. I propose that there are five false identity temptations that live in the culture of toxic reactivity which we have been considering. Why do I call them false identity temptations? Because they function to make you conclude things about yourself that are not true and, because they do, they are not only deceptive but also powerfully seductive.

Attention

For all of us, the attention of other people tends to have far more power than it should. We are wired by God to be social beings who are not meant to dwell alone. So our hunger for relationships is not an evil thing but rather a God-created thing. But attaching your identity to the amount of attention you are receiving from others is dangerous. If this is where you get identity, then you begin to do and say things not because they are right, good, loving, kind, moral, or appropriate, but because they garner the attention you seek. If your attention-seeking strategies don't work, then you find yourself depressed and angry, but you will try even harder to get the identity you're seeking.

Imagine that attention is where you get your identity, security, and inner sense of well-being and you're at a party. Whether or not you're conscious of what you're doing, you will do things at the party that draw attention to yourself. If you succeed, you will leave thinking it was a great party and you will think well of yourself. If your attempts fail and it feels like no one even knew you were there, you will leave depressed and regret that you ever decided to go. Here is the identity power of social media: it allows all of us to draw attention to ourselves. There is power in the number of views or likes. It's why you will post something on Facebook, Instagram, Twitter, or TikTok and then return again and again to see how many likes you've gotten. One of the addicting qualities of social media is its ability to capture attention and thereby feed our identity perception. Sadly more and more of us live to get more and more followers and to get more and more clicks, likes, and views from those who follow us.

All of this social media attention-getting tempts us to behave and communicate in ways that are not good for us or for others. The pride of personal attention and the things we will do to get it are the soil in which toxic reactivity grows. If you post something outrageous that should not be posted, it will get you attention. If you humorously mock someone you should respect, you will get lots of reads. If you mercilessly take someone down, attention will come your way. And if you are looking to social media for identity, you are at least tempted to do these things.

Power

There is something particularly powerful in putting others in their place. You get a buzz of self-righteousness when you take someone down. There is power in having the last word. Why is it more attractive to us to think that we're Jesus with the whip in the temple than it is to follow Jesus in the self-sacrificing love of the cross? There is identity power in proving that you're smarter than the person you're responding to. There is power in thinking that you know more and think better. There is power in thinking that you're on the right side at the moment and on the right side of history. Mockery feels powerful. If you're just the average, unknown person, putting a respected leader in his or her place on Twitter makes you feel like something. And then to have your put-down retweeted by others just adds to the buzz.

But the false identity of social media power is very different from the power of grace-produced character, God-given gifts, surrender to God's call, and a harvest of good fruit that is the result of a life of sacrifice and service. That feeling of power after you've just put someone in his place is the crack cocaine of identity. But it doesn't last long and, because it doesn't, you will be back soon, and you'll be back again and again, getting addicted along the way.

Acceptance

We all want to belong. We all long to be invited in. We all search for groups we can identify with and, when we find such a group, we not only hunger for its acceptance but we do things to get it. None of this is wrong in and of itself, but that acceptance better not be where you get your identity and meaning and purpose. If it is, you'll find yourself doing and saying things that you would not otherwise do and say to get the acceptance that you are seeking. I am persuaded that the toxic tribalism, which is having such negative effects on the church, politics, the function of government, the family, and the health and unity of our local communities, is driven by social media. In a culture where many of us feel alienated, powerless, and alone, the identity of community is a powerful draw. Whether we're aware of it or not, we hunt for a tribe that we can identify with and that will take us in, we take up its cause, and we morph our thinking and communication to whatever standards it may have.

Every time you begin scrolling on your phone, iPad, or laptop, remember that social media is not your church, with trained and godly leadership and a loving, mutually ministering community of faith. Social media is not your family, with seasoned parents who, although imperfect, most often want what's best for you. Social media is not your circle of trusted friends, who really do know you and, if true friends, care about and work toward your welfare. The people in that tribe don't really know you. They don't know if you are happy, sad, depressed, lonely, joyful, or discouraged.

They don't know what hardships you are facing. They don't know the level of your spiritual and emotional vulnerability. They don't know where you might need help. They don't know you. You live in relative anonymity behind the screen. In the true sense of what community means, they are not your community. Social media tribal identity is a mirage that will never replace true community's sturdy love, constant comfort, loving rebuke, commitment to help you bear your burdens, willingness to forgive, acceptance of you, and refusal to abandon you when you mess up.) The hunger that the Creator placed in our hearts, which we all look for, will never be supplied by the backlit screens that seem to dominate our lives.

Moral High Ground

"Moral high ground" was a foundational piece of the identity and toxic legalism of the Pharisees. Jesus powerfully exposed that what the Pharisees thought was moral high ground was a mirage, a false identity. There is a stark difference between true righteousness (the moral high ground that is only ever ours by grace) and prideful self-righteousness. The parable of the Pharisee and the publican in the temple alerts us to the danger of this false identity (Luke 18). It always leads to a distorted self-assessment and a judgmental dismissal of others. A moral high ground spirit will not make you patient, kind, nurturing, understanding, and forgiving. It won't make you listen well and with grace. In the face of someone's inadequacies, weaknesses, and failures, it won't make you reflect on your own. It won't make you assume the best or prevent you from thinking the worst. It will make you quicker to judge than you are to encourage. Moral high ground superiority, with its self-righteousness and judgmental spirit, is a significant accelerant in the fire of toxic reactivity that daily burns away so much of the good that social media could produce. There is a buzz-producing power in thinking that you're more righteous than others, but it's a false identity that will damage both you and the community.

Control

Leaving a conversation, digital or otherwise, that you have controlled can be a heady experience, but it often tempts you to think of yourself in ways that are not true. You may not be as smart as you think you are. You may not communicate as well as you think you do. You may not have the respect of others that you think you have earned. You may have dominated the conversation but, in fact, have little real power. Much of the toxic reactivity on social media is about control. If I post an outrageous response or an over-the-top reaction to you, I entice you to defend yourself or your position. At that point, I am in the driver's seat, now controlling the exchange. Others react against me or they react to defend you or your position. I go after them or their tribe, and the posts are no longer about the original issue but about me. Sadly, sin makes us delight in taking control, even if it's destructive of good communication, healthy community, reputation, respect of another, and the cause of God's kingdom and his righteousness.

The madness of a constant hunt for identity, with all the false identities that such a hunt produces, is graciously and gloriously solved by the gospel. Let's look at some gospel identity passages that are powerful cures for the false-identity temptations that are at the root of much of the toxic reactivity sadly found in the conversations of Christians on social media.

Second Peter 1:3–9 is a diagnostic passage. Peter proposes that there are people who really do know the Lord but whose lives are "ineffective or unfruitful" (1:8). This means their lives are not producing what you would expect the life of a believer to produce—virtue, knowledge, self-control, steadfastness, godliness, brotherly affection, and love (see 1:5–8). Now, when you come across a diagnostic like this in your Bible reading, you ought to ask yourself, "How does this happen? What has caused these people to be 'ineffective or unfruitful'?" The answer is in the next verse. Peter says if someone lacks the qualities of character that make one effective and productive, it is because he "is so nearsighted that he is blind, having forgotten that he was cleansed from his former sins" (1:9). Peter says that if you forget who you are in Christ, you quit pursuing what belongs to you in Christ (the transforming power of grace to progressively renew your character), and you live, relate, and react in ways that are disharmonious with who grace has declared you to be.

And there is more. If you are not getting your identity vertically, you will search for it horizontally, and then you will be susceptible to all kinds of false identity temptations. Looking horizontally for your identity and inner sense of well-being never delivers what you hoped it would; rather, it exposes you to all kinds of sins within and with others along with the (personal and interpersonal damage) that results. This is why your Bible is full of encouraging descriptions of what it means to be a child of God or "in Christ." In Christ we are not only forgiven but we are also given a brand-new identity that protects us from the madness of horizontal identity-seeking and the toxicity it often produces in our digital and face-to-face relationships with others.

First John 3:1–3 is another incredibly helpful and encouraging identity passage:

See what kind of love the Father has given to us, that we should be called the children of God; and so we are. The reason why the world does not know us is that it did not know him. Beloved, we are God's children now, and what we will be has not appeared; but we know that when he appears we shall be like him, because we shall see him as he is. And everyone who thus hopes in him purifies himself as he is pure. (1 John 3:1–3)

This is a "says it all" identity passage. It covers identity past, identity present, and identity future. As God's child, here is your security. Here is your identity. Here is your inner sense of well-being. This is what removes your need to be regularly accepted, affirmed, respected, and agreed with. Here is your freedom from frantically seeking horizontally what you've been given vertically. And here is your freedom from the madness of identity-seeking that fuels so much of the toxic reactivity that lives even in interchanges of Christians on social media. Think about what John is saying. The Creator and Lord of heaven and earth, who rules all things by his wisdom and power, placed his love on you and named you as one of his children. Let it sink in. This means that on your worst day, you are loved. When you feel alienated and alone, you are loved. When others have mocked and dismissed you, you are loved. When the door of human acceptance has been closed to you, you are loved.

"Child of God" is a title you could never have earned or deserved on your own. It is who you are only by the intervention of divine grace. What John is talking about here is not some future hope; it is who you are right now and, because it is, you have been freed by grace from the identity-fear madness that grips so many. But there is more. John says that you can expect that the world won't understand or affirm you because it did not understand or affirm

Jesus. If you are God's child, at the deepest of levels you share identity more fundamentally with your Lord than you do with your neighbor.

Not only was love placed on you in the past and an amazing identity granted you in the present, but your future is secure as well. Finally, John declares that it is personally purifying to rest your identity in the one who planned what needed to be planned, controlled everything that needed to be controlled, and moved inside of you with convicting and empowering grace so that you would become his child. When you place your trust in him and rest in your identity as his child, you are protected from the temptations that come with looking for identity where it can't be found. You're freed from doing and saying things that you should not do or say in order to get attention, power, acceptance, moral superiority, or control. You are able to stand alone. You are able to sustain being misinterpreted and misunderstood. You can stand even being falsely accused or your character being maligned. You don't have to have the loudest voice, control the conversation, or win the day. You are freed from the power-buzz of taking someone down. We should be eternally grateful for the purifying power of our identity as the children of God.

So the next time you sit down with your laptop, grab your iPad, or pull your phone out of your pocket or purse, before you begin to scan your Twitter feed or check out TikTok, stop and remind yourself of who you are by means of glorious adopting grace. Remind yourself of the identity you already have and, because you do, the identities you do not need. Remind yourself that the gospel of justifying, accepting, adopting, and identity-establishing grace is the only lasting curative to the identity madness that propels much of the toxic reactivity that damages so many things that we should hold dear. Speak the psalmist's words to yourself again and again and again; speak them until you are in the forever that is to come and you don't need to speak them anymore: "Though my father and mother forsake me, / the LORD will receive me" (Ps. 27:10 NIV). Here and here alone is where the purifying power of identity security is found.

6

Glory

IT WAS A STUNNING MOMENT of self-glory, but where it took place and how it took place made it even more stark. The man had gone to the temple to pray, but what came out of his mouth was not a prayer (Luke 18:9–14). Well, I guess you could have called it a prayer to himself. Filled with pride at the glory of his own righteousness, he basically told God he didn't need him. He didn't need God's forgiving, transforming, and empowering grace, because he was not like all those other people. Especially like that tax guy over there, weeping and mumbling (the poor guy). No, he was a public religious leader. He knew his religious stuff, he kept the rules, and he deserved all the honor he got. He was in the temple, but he was his own place and object of worship. He was full of himself and, because of that, he saw nearly everyone around him as lesser. He was a religious expert but he was way farther from the God that was at the center of his religious life than he knew. In what is one of the most overt religious acts—prayer—this man stood there as a glory thief, incapable of loving God and incapable of reacting toward those around him with love. There was little that was vertical in his pseudoreligious glory-grabbing. Whatever religious or spiritual trappings he surrounded himself with, the glory of self left no room in his heart for the glory of God.

Self-glory destroys true religion and, because it does, it decimates your ability to then love your neighbor as yourself. Only the one who loves God above all else will ever love his neighbor as himself. Patterns of unloving reactivity toward your neighbor expose an even more tragic thing—a lack of true love for God. In this way, the presence of so much social media self-glory in the conversations of professing Christians reveals a core deficiency that lies at the heart of the culture of the modern evangelical church. Many of us seem obsessed with glory, but it's not the glory of God. No, we're filled with a sense of the glory of our theological knowledge, our biblical literacy, our political conservatism, our social action, the success of our ministries, the number of our followers, who we hang with, the prominence of our tribe, and the power of our ability to communicate. And we're thankful that we are not like other people who don't have what we have. We are righteous, we are experts, and we know what's best. This kind of self-glory will always blind your eyes to the humility, gratitude, and love-producing glory of God.

The culture of toxic reactivity that seems to have taken over not only social media but much of the social landscape of our daily lives is not first a horizontal problem. It's not first about how to respond lovingly to my neighbor. It's more deeply about a war that rages in the heart of every sinner between the glory of self and the glory of God. It is there where we must focus our battle against toxic reactivity if real lasting change is ever going to take place. This great spiritual war exposes the depth of our need for divine rescue. In many ways this is exactly what the gospel of Jesus Christ is all about. The gospel narrative, which is Scripture's dominant theme, unfolds for us what has gone wrong and how in the world it gets fixed. Social media rules are helpful, but they lack the power to get at the causal factors that produce the toxicity we all encounter every day. We have a heart problem, which horizontal regulations simply do not have the power to solve.

The problem of self-glory, which is one of the things that fuels the fire of toxic reactivity and which is so culture-, community-, and church-destructive, did not begin with social media. Social media is the huge influential power platform that gives expression to a dark thing that has been around for a very long time. In other words, social media does not *cause* us to respond in a way that is personally and relationally destructive, but the way it is built, the way its platforms operate, and the way its algorithms are designed, *potentiate* an age-old spiritual weakness. Sadly, this is a weakness all of us will carry until sin is no more. Let me explain how the gospel exposes and offers the solution to the problem of self-glory and all of the relational toxicity that results from it.

Let me take you back before the invention of the internet, the invention of the computer, the invention of the television, and the invention of the radio. Let me take you back millennia before even the printing press was invented. We find ourselves at the first recorded human conversation in a very simple world that was about to become deeply and tragically complicated (Gen. 3). The world of Genesis 1 and 2 was gloriously simple. Everything was perfectly created, everything was in its perfectly designed place, and everything did exactly what it was intended to do all of the time. It was a simple world of peace and harmony, totally without dysfunction, acrimony, brokenness, or toxicity of any kind. As I have been writing this book, a longing has grown in my heart to live in a world like that of Genesis 1 and 2.

But this world didn't last long. Adam and Eve decided to step across God's holy, wise, and loving boundaries. Their disobedience was sin rooted in self-glory. What hooked Adam and Eve was the seductive lie that if they ate the forbidden fruit, they would be like God. Sin is always rooted in glory thievery and, because it is, the sin of Adam and Eve ushered into the world a glory war. Consequently, this war causes all of us to somehow, someway abandon our allegiance to the glory of God and to live for the glory of self. But glory thievery never remains just a vertical thing; it also carries with it destructive horizontal results. Adam and Eve don't just hide in guilt and shame from God; they also experience shame and acrimony between one another. And the destructive results of self-glory don't just stay with Adam and Eve but are carried on in their sons. Cain is so eaten with jealousy toward his brother, whose sacrifice was accepted by God while his was rejected, that he murdered his brother in envious rage. Jealousy and envy, the inability to celebrate the blessing or success of another because it is not our own, is rooted in self-glory. Adam and Eve's glory thievery creates a relational toxicity that gets very dark, very fast.

Every moment of cruel mockery on social media, every attempt to completely cancel someone, every time more and more people pile on, every dismissal, every unfounded judgment of motives and character, every straw man argument, and every tribal attack is rooted in self-glory. Each of these is about taking power, being recognized, and being smarter and more insightful or righteous in some way. These reactions are spotlight stealing, not from another person but from God. These responses do not flow from a commitment to give God glory, but rather are about the seductive buzz of the self-aggrandizing moment. Self-glory never produces patient love, forgiving grace, humble respect, a willingness to listen, or a

84

commitment to guard another's reputation in your relationships. Self-glory never makes you kinder, more tender, or more gentle. Self-glory turns truth into a weapon and uses words to harm. If every brother or sister in Christ reacted on social media or in (face-to-face relationships) with the glory of God in view, the toxic reactivity that sadly lives in both domains would be no more.

Because toxic reactivity, which is so destructive to the community that is essential to the health of human existence, has its roots in self-glory, I want to use a self-glory narrative from the Bible to see how self-glory operates. There is no better place to look to understand the operation of self-glory than the story of Nebuchadnezzar in the book of Daniel. Nebuchadnezzar was king of Babylon, a great warrior, and the conquering king of the kingdom of Judah. But with all of his power and all of his conquests, Nebuchadnezzar was obsessed with his own glory, so much so that he demanded worship. God was about to take Nebuchadnezzar down, but before he did, he warned him in a confusing and mysterious dream. Daniel was tasked with interpreting the king's dream, and it is in the interpretation and Nebuchadnezzar's response to it that we see how self-glory operates. Here is God's appeal, through Daniel, to Nebuchadnezzar: "Therefore, O king, let my counsel be acceptable to you: break off your sins by practicing righteousness, and your iniquities by showing mercy to the oppressed" (Dan. 4:27). I don't know if you saw it as you read this verse, but Daniel restates the vertical and horizontal requirements of the two Great Commandments. He is exhorting Nebuchadnezzar to do these things precisely because the king's life and rule had been shaped by the exact opposite. Self-glory decimates the two Great Commandments. If you're living for your own glory, you will not love God above anything else by doing what is right in his eyes, and you will not love your neighbor as yourself by being committed to mercy wherever it is needed. Self-glory means I do what pleases me, and I really don't care about the plight of others.

But there is more. Twelve months after this exhortation we find Nebuchadnezzar on the balcony of his palace. Let me just say as an aside that this is to me an amazing picture of the patient grace of the Lord. He had given the king twelve months to decide whether or not he was going to repent. Twelve months! If you're a parent, can you imagine saying to your child, "Your room is a constant mess. I want you to give it a thorough cleaning, and you have twelve months to get it done"? God's patience with Nebuchadnezzar should be an encouragement to us all. But listen to what Nebuchadnezzar says as he looks out over his kingdom: "Is not this great Babylon, which I have built by my mighty power as a royal residence and for the glory of my majesty?" (Dan. 4:30). Self-glory will cause you to take credit for what you could not have earned or produced on your own. All of the king's power, military brilliance, physical strength, success, and even his life and breath came from the Lord. But to Nebuchadnezzar it was all a monument to one thing: his glory.

Here is the way self-glory operates. It causes me to do what I do for no greater purpose than that it pleases me. It causes me to be so busy loving myself that I have little time and energy to love others, and it makes me take personal credit for what I could never do or produce on my own. Think of how these three things operate when self-glory meets Twitter, Facebook, TikTok, or Instagram. I come loaded with my own glory. I post whatever it is that gives me pleasure. I am not sensitive to how what I post may affect others. I come to social media feeling entitled and deserving because of who I am, what I've done, what I know, or maybe simply because of the amount of followers I have attracted. I post what will get me the most likes because I am motivated by my own glory, no matter how proud, outrageous, or hurtful. If it makes me feel good to mock or dismiss, then I will. If taking someone down gives me pleasure, then that is what I'll do. I don't post for the benefit of others; even if I think I do, every post is really for me because the motivating drive that is in possession of my heart is self-glory, and it will exercise inescapable influence over my reactions.

I am convinced that many of the theological battles on Twitter are motivated not by a love for theology after all but by self-glory. When ruling your heart, the truths of the word of God will never produce cruel mockery, angry accusations, or a willingness to judge motives or assail another's character. Using words to harm is not the fruit of good theology. Theology that does not produce love is simply bad, God-dishonoring, and unbiblical theology. The desire to be a social media truth vigilante is not motivated by God's honor and glory or his magnificent truth but by self-glory. Self-glory often masquerades as a fight for what is right. If you find pleasure in the battle and you love the kill, it's probably not God's glory that's driving you, because he is slow to anger and lavish in love. If tenderness, gentleness, kindness, patience, and love seem like weakness to you, it's doubtful that the glory of God is shaping how you act, react, and respond. I think the toxic reactivity of Christians—often toward other Christians—on social media is a constant warning to us that the kingdom of self does a good job of masquerading as the kingdom of God. May we be humble enough to search our hearts. Perhaps as we post, it is not God we're serving after all.

The Solution to the Toxicity

I want to end this chapter with an examination of a passage that points us to the only solution to the glory war that often rages in our hearts and the beautiful fruit that this solution will produce in our lives. This passage reminds us that the cure for toxic reactivity, which is the focus of this book, is found in something deeper and more fundamental than a new set of social media regulations or in limiting your use of these platforms (which is probably a very good idea). Written thousands of years before the birth of these incredibly powerful platforms of communication that have become so divisive and harmful, Psalm 112 is right on topic:

> Praise the LORD!
> Blessed is the man who fears the LORD,
>   who greatly delights in his commandments! . . .
> Light dawns in the darkness for the upright;
>   he is gracious, merciful, and righteous.
> It is well with the man who deals generously and lends;
>   who conducts his affairs with justice.
> For the righteous will never be moved;
>   he will be remembered forever.
> He is not afraid of bad news;
>   his heart is firm, trusting in the LORD. (Ps. 112:1, 4–7)

First, Psalm 112 offers to believers the only lasting solution to the toxic reactivity madness that has captured and distorted much of the dialogue of the church. Fear of the Lord is the solution. The psalmist is not talking here of a terror that would make me want to run away and hide from the Lord, but rather an awe-inspiring recognition of his power and glory that would make me run to him, rest in him, and be willing to surrender to his will for me. This fear alone quiets all the other fears and motivations that make up the nasty stew of toxicity that is so daily damaging. When fear of the Lord has captured my heart, I don't fear what other people will think of me, how my words will be received, or a thousand other "what ifs" that could capture my heart. When I am living in a functional awe of God and his power, glory, and grace, and when I am blown away that one of such incalculable glory would include me in his family, I will not be impressed by my own glory. If God's glory is what motivates me, then self-glory, with all of its desire for power, acclaim, control, recognition, and moral high ground, won't.

Then Psalm 112 details for us the gorgeous fruit in the life of the person who lives in a heart-capturing and life-shaping fear of the Lord. The person who fears the Lord will be "gracious, merciful, and righteous" (112:4). Imagine if these three character qualities were to shape everything you post and every conversation you have. Imagine if every reaction that every Christian typed into his phone were gracious, merciful, and righteous. Think about the impact that would have on the media landscape that we traverse every day. The person who fears the Lord is not disrespectful, angry, or vengeful but rather generous, one who conducts his affairs with justice. Justice deals with evil in a way that does not create more evil. Generosity is not just a financial thing but also a giving and serving spirit in every area of your life, including your communication. Generous people listen well, give you the benefit of the doubt, and endeavor to think the best of you. Generous people aren't stingy with patience, love, sympathy, understanding, and grace. Generous people don't use words as weapons; no, their words are used as gifts, (meant to relieve, encourage, clarify, instruct, comfort, and edify.)

Finally, the psalm says that when fear of the Lord rules your heart, you are (not afraid of bad news.) You don't live afraid of the next attack, the next time you will be misunderstood, the next time your character or qualifications are called into question. Fear of the Lord will keep you from always looking for the next enemy around the corner. Fear of the Lord means you are getting your security and peace not from how people are responding to you, but from who the Lord is and from what he has done and is doing for you. I so appreciate how the psalmist talks about this security and rest. He says "his heart is firm" (Ps. 112:7). Firmness of heart, which is only ever the fruit of fear of the Lord, will rescue you from becoming part of the toxic madness that is such a destructive force in our current communication culture. I am afraid that many believers have wobbly hearts. They lack the firmness of rest, security, and peace that comes from awe of the glorious glory of the Lord. When your heart is wobbly, whether you know it or not you are searching horizontally for a stability of heart and mind that can only be found vertically. So you demand recognition, respect, appreciation, power, control, and this list goes on. You demand these things because they give you a feeling of firmness for a moment, but it never lasts. In your "I must have this," you fail to hear people well, you fail to love them well, and you fail to give them the grace that everyone always needs. You may think you're standing for what is right, but what you're actually doing is demanding what you want and think you deserve. It's all driven by a heart that is not at rest and, because it isn't, you fail to be gracious, righteous, and merciful.

Psalm 112, ancient though it is, is right on topic. It reinforces the main theme of this book: the gospel exposes the roots of and the only lasting solution to the toxic reactivity that distorts and damages the communication culture that is both outside and within the body of Christ. You may be a believer. You may have a high level of theological understanding and biblical literacy. You may have walked with the Lord for a while. You may have ministry experience. But I ask you to open your heart to this question: Could it be that there is a whole lot of self-glory still living in your heart? Are there times when you proudly flash your theological knowledge, like some badge you have earned? Do you at times use it as a weapon and not a gift that serves? Do you look down on those who seem less knowledgeable or less insightful than you? Do you go looking for a fight or jump too quickly into someone else's fight? Are you demanding, entitled, overcritical? Do you hear your opponents well? Do you give them grace? Do you treat them with dignity and respect? Are you quick to admit when you are wrong or have treated someone wrongly? Are your words measured, careful, and crafted to do good? Could it be that you're not actually defending the glory of God and his truth but rather projecting, defending, and protecting your own glory?

I wish I could say that self-glory never motivates me, but I can't. I wish I could say that fear of the Lord is always more powerful and influential in my heart than any other fear, but I can't. So I invite you to do what I endeavor to do every morning. I invite you, before you begin your busy day, to take a few moments to focus the eyes of your heart on the stunning glory of the Lord and the awesome glory of his grace. Each morning allow your self-glory to melt in the redeeming heat of divine glory. Allow fear of the Lord to disarm every other fear. And as you bask in the splendor of the glorious beauty of who he is, plead with your Lord to rescue you from you throughout the day. Then get up and determine to keep his glory in view, in every conversation, whether digital or personal. And then look for opportunities to be gracious, merciful, righteous, and generous. Jesus lived, died, and rose again so these characteristics would be our potential. May each of us speak and post with God's glory in view. His grace makes this possible.

7

Eternity

I DON'T KNOW IF YOU'VE NOTICED it or not, but there are no spoiler alerts in the Bible. God puts the final chapter, the final end of all things, and the forever that will follow before us throughout his narrative. He does this so that we will interpret the entire content of his marvelous revelation to us with eternity in view. And he does this so that eternity would shape how we live in the situations, locations, and relationships of our daily lives. God intends for us to live eschatologically, and when we fail to do that, bad things happen. You will never live the way you were designed to live if you fall into thinking that this moment is all you have to be sure of. So God, in the goodness of his grace and the practicality of his wisdom, invites us to look into and eavesdrop on eternity.

Now this is yet another place where the gospel helps us to understand and properly guard ourselves against the toxic reactivity that distorts so many conversations, harms so many lives, and damages the witness of the church. I am persuaded that much of the toxicity that we daily deal with, not just outside of the Christian community but inside of it as well, is the result of a subtle but widespread epidemic of eternity amnesia. Sure, every believer has the doctrine of eternity as part of his confessional theology. Every Christian believes in eternal life, but not nearly as many live with eternity in view. And not many understand that when you do, it changes the way you react to everything in your life. God unfolds the final chapter for us not just so we'll be prepared, but so that we will know how to live right here, right now. So let's view our reactivity culture through the lens of eternity.

Eternity as Teacher

The first and perhaps most foundational thing the biblical teaching of eternity does is give us a hermeneutical tool for making sense out of our lives. I have written and spoken much about the fact that every human being is an interpreter. We all live, act, react, and respond based not on the facts of our experience but based on our particular interpretation of the facts. Hermeneutics is the science of interpretation and, for Christians who have built their lives on the truths of God's word, eternity is a very important interpretive tool. Truth of the eternity that is to come alerts us to the fact that the Bible is much more than a set of truths to be read, understood, believed, and defended. The Bible is a narrative, that is, the ultimate grand story. The Bible has a main character, the Lord Almighty, it has a plotline, and it has a conclusion that is glorious beyond description.

Living as a Bible believer means much more than getting your doctrine right and searching for those who seek to reshape or negate it in some way. Living as a Bible believer means embedding your story in the larger story of redemption. If you're God's child, then his story, by grace, is your story. His presence and power are your hope; where the story is going is where your story is going, and the final victory at the end is your victory too. The Bible is rich with counsel on how to live in the middle of the plot of God's story, because we live in the messiness between the promise of the glories that are to come and the actual arrival of those glories. Eternity comforts us with one amazing truth: everything is going to be okay because God is going to make all things new again. So, we don't need to live in a state of panic. We don't have to fear that the enemies of what is right will ultimately win. We don't have to ride the rollercoaster of all the ups and downs and twists and turns of the unsettled mind of the culture around us. We don't have to be political vigilantes who think that political leaders will guide us to the hope and security we seek. We don't have to fear what others think of us, how much they misunderstand us, or how aggressively they react to us. We know who we are, we know what we have been graced to be part of, we know where God is taking us, and we know how it is all going to end. We are in the middle of an unstoppable grace narrative, and it will be okay.

Could it be that much of the fearful, defensive, angry, and anxious reactivity that lives in the Christian community and in our social media conversation is the result of a God's-story forgetfulness? Could it be that we have lost sense of the plot? Could it be that we've reduced the most precious story ever written, the only one that can give life to the dead, into a set of truths to be argued about? Could it be that we have lost sight of what the biblical story tells about where true and lasting hope, security, identity, and rest can be found? The pastors I mentor have told me again and again that the angry reactivity which now lives in their congregations is driven by fear. What if our liberties are taken away? What if this leader doesn't win? What if my pastor isn't politically conservative? What if this view of gender wins the day? What if this conspiracy is true? I am deeply persuaded that much of the toxicity that is interrupting and corrupting our communication, our relationships, our ministries, and our witness is driven by a God's-plot amnesia, and the result of this amnesia is fear.

Fearful people come to family gatherings, to church, to elections, and to social media defensive and loaded. We seem to be way too fearful and way too ready to react in an instant. And we appear to have forgotten that we have been included in a divinely instituted movement that cannot and will not be stopped. God will win, and his children will celebrate that victory with him and share in its spoils.

Eternity and Values

Not only does the biblical truth of the eternity that is to come provide us with a way of making sense out of and living within the messiness of the middle of God's great story, it also provides us with a much needed values clarification. I find myself going back again and again to Jesus's teaching in Matthew 6. This is one of the most significant values passages in all of Scripture. Here Christ uses a provocative word for the values that come to control our hearts. He calls them *treasures* (Matt. 6:19). The word paints the scene of a chest of gold and jewels. A treasure is something that rises in importance in your heart until it controls what you think, what you desire, and how you act. Jesus is alerting us to the fact that we are all treasure oriented, that is, we all live for some kind of treasure. But this word confronts us with something else. Most of the treasures we come to value and that end up controlling us are not things of intrinsic value but assigned value. Think of a twenty-dollar bill. It's not worth twenty dollars because it is twenty dollars' worth of ink or paper. The paper bill itself doesn't have intrinsic value, but it does have assigned value, value assigned by the Department of the Treasury. So, you can take your twenty-dollar bill to the grocery store and buy twenty dollars' worth of food.

Christ is warning us that we will have treasures and they will control our hearts and, because they do, they will shape our words and behavior. But he is also alerting us that many of the things we have named as treasures are not so valuable after all because they lack true, intrinsic, or eternal value. It is here where eavesdropping on eternity can be so helpful in clarifying values. When you listen to the celebrations of the saints on the other side, it's important to take note of what they are celebrating. The constant theme of the eternal celebration is God—the awesomeness of his power, the finality of his victory, and his generous grace along the way. No one in eternity will be celebrating how big their house was, how successful their career was, or how much money they had. No one will be celebrating how many debates they won, how influential their tribe was, how many social media followers they had, how many important leaders they took down, how their political movement won, or how successful they were at defending encroachments on their personal rights. No one.

Could it be that proving we are right has become more important to us than living and reacting in a way that is right? Could it be that political movements are too important to us? Could it be that secondary issues, those that have been and will always be debated, have become too important to us? Could it be that theological-always-rightism has become too much of a heart-controlling treasure to us? Could it be that we treasure winning more than loving, controlling more than serving, and judgment more than encouragement? Jesus tells us in Matthew 6 what is truly valuable: his kingdom and his righteousness. Could it be that we have lost our minds when it comes to what is really worth living and fighting for? Could it be that if we live inside of the warnings of Matthew 6 and the values of Revelation, much of the fearful and toxic reactivity that lives in the church and in the conversations of Christians on social media would be no more? Everything you text, email, speak, or post reveals the true values of your heart. Since this is true, it is important to confess that there is daily evidence in our churches and on the internet that we have lost the plot of what is truly valuable, truly worth giving our hearts to, and truly worth living for.

Eternity and Rest

Eternity gives us one more thing: lasting spiritual rest. Reactivity never comes from hearts at rest. It simply doesn't. Rest of heart comes when you are blown away by the fact that your destiny is unalterably secure. If you are guaranteed this future grace, then you are guaranteed present grace as well. Without present grace you would never make it to receive the future grace that is yours in Christ. A restful heart is the product of gratitude. When your heart is filled with gratitude, it alters the way you see your world, it changes the way you experience each day, it shapes the way you see other people, and it changes the way you understand and deal with difficulty. When your heart is at rest, you aren't easily irritated, you aren't overcritical, you aren't gunning for a fight, you don't personalize things that are not personal, and you aren't frantically looking for acceptance or devastated when you don't get it.

On the other hand, a life of forgetfulness, ingratitude, and complaint will unsettle your heart. It will cause you to be weaker and less resilient. It will cause you to be irritable and critical. Complaint means you are dissatisfied and, because you are, you will find more reason to be dissatisfied. You will be quicker to get angry, quicker to take offense, and less patient with others. Complaining people don't have much joy and aren't quick to sympathize with the plight of others and extend mercy to them.

The tone and character of much of the social media conversation in the current cultural setting depicts a whole lot of personal, relational, and cultural unrest, but so does the social media conversation of believers. The church, which should be an earthly picture of the rest that is to come, is clearly now a place of spiritual unrest. Complaint seems to speak more loudly than praise. We are too easily angered. We are too easily offended. We are too easily politicized and tribalized. We seem to lack patient empathy, a willingness to think the best of others, and the commitment to be slow to judge motives or question one's character. Have we lost sight of the unstoppable and eternal grace that is ours in Christ? Have we forgotten how important it is to count our blessings? If the eternity that is ours in Christ, along with all the gifts of grace along the way, doesn't capture your heart and make you overflow with gratitude, then you will find it very hard to resist the toxic reactivity that seems to be everywhere you look. As God's people, we are in desperate need of a gratitude revival and the vertical and horizontal rest that results.

Rejoice and Be Reasonable

Philippians 4:4–7 speaks to everything we have been considering:

> Rejoice in the Lord always; again I will say, rejoice. Let your reasonableness be known to everyone. The Lord is at hand; do not be anxious about anything, but in everything by prayer and supplication with thanksgiving let your requests be made known to God. And the peace of God, which surpasses all

understanding, will guard your hearts and your minds in Christ
Jesus. (Phil. 4:4–7)

This important and helpful passage makes a direct connection
between the present condition of our hearts and the future coming of the Lord. It also connects gratitude ("rejoicing always")
to the way we respond to literally everyone. "Let your reasonableness be known to everyone" is a power-packed sentence. If
taken seriously and lived out with discipline, it would alter the
Christian social media landscape for good. The original Greek
word that we translate as "reasonableness" is a multilayered and
provocative word which is almost impossible to translate with a
single English word. It carries the meaning of patience, gentleness, softness, modesty, magnanimity, moderation, and forbearance. If these traits were to control our hearts as we sit down
with our phones, tablets, and computers, we would no longer
be part of a reactivity culture. God has given us everything we
need to be free of anxiety, to be filled with thankfulness, and
to have hearts that are protected by peace, so that we would
be known for our gentle and forbearing reasonableness. This is
a game-changer passage. Paul is not giving us his opinion on
how nice it would be to be nice. No, he is confronting us with
the truth that if we meditate on everything we have been given
and on our inclusion in the glories that are to come, this then
is how we should live. It's wrong not to rejoice. It's wrong not
to be thankful. Something is wrong if you are not experiencing
peace of heart. And it is wrong if your reactions to everyone
are less than gentle, forbearing, and reasonable. These are the
foundational character qualities of gospel living, and they are
made possible for us by grace.

Something is wrong if these glorious truths produce in us big theological brains, proud and judgmental hearts, and reactions to others that lack gentle, patient reasonableness. A heart filled with gospel gratefulness will not produce a Twitter, Instagram, or Facebook troll. A heart that is resting in present and future grace won't be easily dissatisfied or quickly critical. A heart that is filled with thanksgiving will use words to edify, comfort, and encourage, not to slay the next, nearest enemy. But gospel amnesia, which forgets what we have been given now and what is guaranteed to come, leaves us vulnerable to the seductive call of the reactivity culture that has drawn and continues to draw too many of us in.

Make Use of Your Time

One last thing. The existence of the eternity that is to come calls for all of us to use our time well. As we are waiting for the sure return of our Lord and the establishment of his final kingdom, there will be a rise of false prophets and all the evils that result (see Matt. 24:11–12). While we wait in this broken and groaning world, we are not hopeless, anxious, angry, or fear-ridden. And we surely are not passive. As we have already been considering, we are told how to live. Ephesians 5:16 tells us: "Making the best use of the time, because the days are evil." This needed and helpful directive comes in the middle of a section of counsel on how to live between the "already" and the "not yet." Unfortunately, this passage is regularly misunderstood and misapplied. The confusion has to do with the word *time*. Paul is not using the word *time* in a chronological sense, like "hurry up, we don't have much time." He is using the word *time* in a point-in-time sense. He is directing the Ephesians believers, and us, to make the best use of *this time*. His counsel to believers is to capture all the opportunities that God will give them to live as children of light in a darkened world, to display the glory of God in a world obsessed with other glories, to show forth God's truth in a world captured by falsehood, and to resist temptation in a world where so many give way to its seduction.

The point of this passage is that as we embrace the hope that is to come, we have a calling. We are to live, act, and respond with a sense of mission. We are called to a greater purpose than whatever our purpose would be for ourselves. We have not just been invited into God's family, but we have been drafted into his mission on earth. We are to actively live with a commitment to the greatest, most important movement in human history—redemption. We are to live for things that are eternal and transcendent. We should never view the world through the small lens of what we have or don't have, how we are or are not being responded to, what is or is not making us uncomfortable, or what we do or do not think we deserve. We must not allow ourselves to shrink the field of our concern, motivation, or reactions down to the size of our little lives. We have been welcomed to something infinitely greater, and we have been called to live with these things in view. Toxic reactivity is the result of a life shrunk down to the size of our wants, our needs, and our feelings. It is about making ourselves more important than we are and our opinions more significant than they should ever be.

In a moment of toxic reactivity, there is no past, there is no future, there is no grand glorious movement, and there is no transcendent mission. As we are taking someone down in ridicule, mockery, and dismissal, we have forgotten who we are and the grand thing that we have been called to do. We have lost sight of the fact that we are children of light in the midst of darkness, and we have sadly become part of the dark reactivity of a world gone mad. When we put our fingers on our keyboards and let it rip, we have forsaken the call that is on us to capture every opportunity to point to God's glory and the eternal hope of his grace. When winning becomes more important, our tribe more significant, and the takedown more fulfilling than God's work is, we have lost our gospel minds and forgotten that our little stories have been embedded by grace in the transcendent story of the glory of God, his redeeming grace, and the eternity of peace and righteousness that is ours as his children.

May God give us the grace to live, act, and react in light of the mercies that we have already been given and the glories that are to come. May he help us to make the most of the opportunities he will give us. And may our gentle and patient reasonableness be evident in every conversation, every reaction, and every post, because it really is true that the Lord is near.

8

Selflessness

SELF GETS IN THE WAY, constantly inserting itself and making things more difficult than they would otherwise be. It turns relationships into a minefield; you never know when you're going to step on the wrong thing. It turns words into weapons, blessings into entitlements, and desires into demands. It makes you self-excusing while being critical and judgmental when it comes to the other guy. It makes dissatisfaction a regular state of being and gratitude rare. It finds reasons to be unhappy and takes credit way too often. It is a state of self-importance that weakens your ability to put yourself in anyone else's place. It makes you love power and control, and it makes you see serving as burdensome. It makes you think too much about how you feel, how you feel about how you feel, and how you feel about how others respond to how you feel. It tricks you into thinking that you're more of an expert than you actually are, while you resist the expertise of others. It causes you to think that your experience is *the* experience, while you discount the experiences of others. It makes everything personal; everything is about you somehow, someway. It causes you to speak a lot and listen little. It is life caving in on itself, a dysfunctional and dissatisfying existence. It is the opposite of the way things were meant to be, the opposite of the way we were created to live.

This sad way of living is called *selfishness*. Note how I am using this word. I don't just mean that you are not a very giving person because you want everything for yourself. What I mean by this word is that the driving motivation for everything in your life is self. You are at the center of your world. You do what you do and say what you say for your own purpose and pleasure. You are what motivates you. You are what makes you happy. You are your goal. You are fundamentally self-aware and self-possessed. Your foundational lifestyle is selfish, no matter who you think you are and what you say you believe.

It needs to be said and repeated often, particularly in our current cultural setting, that there is no idol more attractive, seductive, and deceptive than the *idol of self*. You could argue that every act of disregard of the commands, commitments, and wisdom principles of Scripture is rooted and motivated by the worship of self. This is what drove the first act of disobedience in the garden and continues to cause us to step over God's boundaries today. This is why Paul says that Jesus came so that those who live would no longer live "for themselves" (see 2 Cor. 5:14–15). When worship of self functionally replaces worship of God, you simply will not live, act, react, and respond as God intended and has commanded. A failure to obey God's commands is never just a breaking of some abstract moral code; it is a breaking of the worship relationship you were created to have with the Lord of lords. Every act of disobedience is a denial of God's rightful place and an insertion of yourself into his place. This is why David, having committed adultery and murder said, "Against you, you only, have I sinned / and done what is evil in your sight" (Ps. 51:4). Every act of hatred, cruelty, dismissal, disrespect, violence, prejudice, and harm against one of God's image bearers is ignited and fueled by the worship of the idol of self.

But, you may ask, what does this have to do with the church, which is full of people who have given their lives to the Lord? Well, if the DNA of sin is the worship of self, and if all of our sins have been forgiven but not yet fully eradicated, then there will still be artifacts of the old worship of self within us. All of us have to deal with the temptation of selfism every day, whether that is getting mad at someone who has disagreed with us, or angry at the drivers who are in our way in traffic, or impatient with children who need parenting at an inopportune time, or envious that a friend is enjoying blessings that we would like for ourselves, or simply doing what pleases us instead of what God says is right for us. As long as sin still lives inside of us, there will be a problem of selfism in the Christian community. This is why there is so much conflict in the church. Few of the struggles within the church are purely about things of biblical or theological consequence. It is self-importance that causes us to have trouble living with and ministering alongside of one another. Minor offenses, petty quarrels, desires for recognition, and battles for control get in the way of the life and mission that God has called us to. Yes, in the community of faith the worship of God collides with the worship of self. One of the evidences of this is the culture of toxic reactivity that lives on our social media sites and in the conversations of Christians, who have been called to the following lifestyle: "With all humility and gentleness, with patience, bearing with one another in love, eager to maintain the unity of the Spirit in the bond of peace" (Eph. 4:2–3). If we loved this way—God's way—more than we loved our own way, this culture of toxicity would disappear.

Jesus knew what still lived in the hearts of all who would follow him. That's why he said, "If anyone would come after me, let him *deny himself* and take up his cross daily and follow me" (Luke 9:23). The foundational command of Christian living is self-denial. Selflessness is the platform on which every other aspect of Christian, biblical discipleship stands. The call to humility, gentleness, patience, service, forgiveness, generosity, unity, and love requires self-denial. Without selflessness there will never be a surrender to a greater agenda than my own. It is selflessness that causes me to use the things in my life as resources to love the people in my life, rather than using people to get the things that I want. This selfless living is not possible outside of the transformative power of God's grace. In order to live this way, I need to be rescued from me, and not just once, but again and again. This why John says, "For from his fullness we have all received, grace upon grace" (John 1:16). I don't need one infusion of grace; I need infusions of the spiritual chemotherapy of God's grace again and again until the cancer of self-worship no longer lives in my heart. That day is coming, but until then, my hope and yours is "grace upon grace." Think of the disciples of Jesus. They had left everything to follow him, yet right after Jesus told them of his soon-to-come suffering and death, they commenced to argue about who would be greatest in the kingdom (see Mark 9:33–37).

So it is important for us to be humbly honest about the roots of toxicity that live in our churches, the wider Christian community, and in our internet conversations. The conversations that are needed about important cultural, political, theological, biblical, and ecclesiastical issues will become dark, hurtful, and divisive when self is at the center. It takes selflessness to patiently listen to and consider another's perspective. It takes selflessness to respond lovingly and respectfully. It takes selflessness to avoid judgments of character and motivation. It takes selflessness to care more about the reputation of your Savior than how you are being responded to. It takes selflessness to find more joy in encouraging than in condemning. It takes selflessness to forgive, restore, and reconcile. It take selflessness to debate in a way that preserves unity. It takes selflessness to treat someone you disagree with as a brother or sister. It takes selflessness to care more about the mission of your Master than the number of clicks or followers you're getting. It takes selflessness to admit you were wrong, you misjudged a person, or you misunderstood a post. And it takes grace to be selfless at any time and in any way. It is time for us all to cry out for that grace. And as we do, it's important for us to remember that God has promised that when we cry, he will hear and answer.

The Culture of Self and Toxic Reactivity

What happens to our personal and digital conversations when self is at the center? They become dark and toxic. Let me detail how this happens and what it looks like.

The culture of self causes people to be *too easily offended.* When you are in the center of your world, somehow, someway you make everything about you. Your life is about who notices you or who does not, who agrees with you and who doesn't, who respects you and who doesn't, how much you are heard or ignored, whether your side is winning or not, or whether you're taken seriously or not. It is *meism* gone wild. Because life is all about you, you are always looking for a personal offense, whether you realize it or not. So you will invariably personalize what is not personal and, because you do, you will be adversarial in your response, which will usually get the same in return. This will reinforce your feelings of personal attack and seem to validate the very personal way you experience things. Because you are always on the lookout, you will find offense where there is no offense and hurt where there is no hurt. A few words posted or a look on someone's face will have the power to offend you and set you off. Contrast this with the peace of heart and peace in your relationships that result when your life is about love of God and love of neighbor, rather than being all about you. Such is the selfless culture to which all of God's children have been called.

Because life really is all about you, *you will be too in love with your own opinion.* Romans 12:3 calls us to refrain from thinking of ourselves more highly than we ought to think. Many of us simply hold what we think in too high regard. We are too proudly content with what we think—not because it's biblical but because we think it. We are too sure of being sure and we feel too right about always being right. We are too ready to have an opinion on everything and too ready to assume that our opinion is the opinion that everyone should have. We are too quick to assess that we are wise and surrounded by those who are less than wise. We love to hear ourselves talk or read our own post, while we impatiently tolerate the responses of others. Because we are too in love with our opinion, it is hard for us to be good students, hard for us to learn what we don't already know, and hard for us to hear from those who know more or better. We have forgotten the sad fact that sin reduces all of us to fools and that as long as sin still lives in our hearts, artifacts of foolishness will remain. Selfless living recognizes that there is only one who is perfectly and faithfully wise all the time and in every way and that all of the rest of us need to be daily rescued by the grace of his wisdom, no matter how long we have sat at his feet.

When you are in the center of your world and too in love with your own thinking, *it is hard for you to handle disagreement*. I have seen how topical, theological, or political debates quickly escalate into heated arguments that often turn personal. When this happens, it tells you a lot more about the debaters than it does about the topic being debated. If you go into a conversation remembering that you are still a sin-flawed person, capable of being wrong, always needing to learn, and in constant need of God's rescuing grace, you will be open to consider opinions, perspectives, and interpretations that are different from your own. And if you believe in the sovereign and loving care of your Redeemer, you will be open to him putting someone in your path to interrupt your private conversation, to make you think about things you would have never thought about on your own, and to bring you to new insights, understandings, and commitments. If it is practically impossible for you to think that you're incapable of flawed thinking, then any disagreement will be taken as a personal offense, and rather than having a respectful debate with those who disagree with you, you will tend to attack them personally. The selfless person holds his thinking with an open hand. Even when he is holding on to biblical truth, he is willing to admit that he may be holding it improperly or out of balance, always being ready to learn and grow. Spend time on social media and you'll begin to wonder how many humble, selfless learners there are out there.

If you are in the center of your world, too confident and too sure, *you will tend to resist correction*. It make sense, doesn't it? If you're sure that your thinking is nearly always right, then you don't think that you're a person in need of correction. You will tend to see yourself as the corrector rather than the one needing correction. You will always be trolling for the next poor soul who needs correction whether you're conscious of it or not. You will not live in the humility of knowing that you have not arrived but are on the pathway to maturity of character and thought. It is humbling to confess that there is nothing in you or about you that is perfect yet and that by grace you are becoming what your Creator designed you to be and what your Savior chose you to be. This means that resisting correction is more than blowing off another person; it is resisting the loving, rescuing, and maturing grace of your Savior. The paradox here is that people who resist correction are the people who most need correction. God has ordained for the body of Christ to have an unending conversation that is mutually edifying, encouraging, comforting, correcting, redirecting, empowering, and motivating. Our Lord, who is committed to his work of correcting grace, uses human tools to continue that work. We all need to humbly hear and consider the rather blunt words of Proverbs 12:1: "Whoever loves discipline loves knowledge, / but he who hates reproof is stupid."

Another dynamic propels the toxic reactivity that seems to be everywhere around us: the self-centered person will tend to *focus more on the sin, weakness, and failures of others than on his own.* You are always in deep spiritual trouble when you are more engaged, grieved, and motivated by the sin or error of others than your own. Is it too easy for you to be irritated by the character flaws of others, while being too tolerant of your own flaws? Does the anger of others bother you more than your own? Do you rail against the prejudice of others, while tolerating your own? Do you love to point out the inconsistencies in others, while being unwilling to examine your own? Do you jump on the weaknesses of others, while being protective of your own? Do you point out potential errors in other theological camps, while never being willing to consider where your camp may be in error? Do you quickly point out where others need to learn, while being unwilling to be taught yourself? Do you work to expose the sin of others, while hiding your own? Is your lifestyle more of a pointed finger than a humble confession? The conversation of Christians on social media often makes it seem as if we're quicker to point the finger and to assign blame than we are to admit wrong, confess our own need to change, and grieve that we still fall below God's holy, righteous, wise, and loving standard. Could it be that much of the toxicity that harms our digital and personal conversations is addressed by Christ's questions in Matthew 7? "Why do you see the speck that is in your brother's eye, but do not notice the log that is in your own eye? Or how can you say to your brother, 'Let me take the speck out of your eye,' when there is the log in your own eye?" (7:3–4). And perhaps we would do much better at protecting ourselves from the toxicity that lives around us if we did what he calls us to do in verse 5: "First take the log out of your own eye, and then you will see clearly to take the speck out of your brother's eye."

If you have put yourself in the center of your world, in the digital or personal community, *you will tend to be a divisive not a unifying presence.* People who make life all about them obviously don't interact with attention to, love for, and appreciation for others. They live with unrealistic expectations (life and people will serve me), so they experience constant disappointment and the anger that follows. Being right, being affirmed, being on the winning side, controlling the conversation, putting people in their place, and getting attention are more important than encouraging the community's unity, understanding, and love.

Making life all about you doesn't lead to unity.
Personalizing what is not personal doesn't lead to unity.
Being adversarial in your reactions doesn't lead to unity.
Not being able to handle disagreement doesn't lead to unity.
Resisting correction doesn't lead to unity.
Too much love for winning doesn't lead to unity.

The key to unity, which the Bible presents as a treasured and essential quality for the family of faith, is selflessness. We find the best presentation of this in Ephesians 4:

> I therefore, a prisoner for the Lord, urge you to walk in a manner worthy of the calling to which you have been called, with all humility and gentleness, with patience, bearing with one another in love, eager to maintain the unity of the Spirit in the bond of peace. There is one body and one Spirit—just as you were called to the one hope that belongs to your call— one Lord, one faith, one baptism, one God and Father of all, who is over all and through all and in all . . . until we all attain to the unity of the faith and of the knowledge of the Son of God, to mature manhood, to the measure of the stature of the fullness of Christ, so that we may no longer be children, tossed to and fro by the waves and carried about by every wind of doctrine, by human cunning, by craftiness in deceitful schemes. Rather, speaking the truth in love, we are to grow up in every way into him who is the head, into Christ, from whom the whole body, joined and held together

by every joint with which it is equipped, when each part is working properly, makes the body grow so that it builds itself up in love. (Eph. 4:1–6, 13–16)

It is important to notice that this passage presents two unities: the unity of the Spirit (4:3) and the unity of the faith (4:13). If we have any hope of reaching the second, we have to be careful to protect and maintain the first. The unity of the Spirit is the divinely created spiritual bond that you and I share with all other believers. This means that no brother or sister in Christ is ever to be viewed as the enemy. No matter how much we may disagree, by the sovereign redemptive plan of God we are in the same family and connected together as members of the same body. The same Spirit that now lives inside of you lives inside of me. And the call in the early verses of this passage is to do everything we can to not damage this unity. How do we do this? The answer in the passage is clear: selfless living. Self-centeredness always disrupts and damages unity.

What does this selfless lifestyle look like? It means being committed to humility, gentleness, patience, forbearance, and peace. If the Christian community, both digital and personal, were functionally committed to these qualities of response, then the toxic reactivity would disappear. Yes, we have a long way to go before we have any semblance of unity in matters of the faith, but the only way to get there is by the selfless, unity-protecting lifestyle that this passage calls us to. Notice the wisdom of the second part of the passage where we are called to speak the truth in love. If we want together to get at the truth, to understand it fully, and to apply it comprehensively, the only pathway that will get us there is love. Truth not spoken in love ceases to be the truth, because it gets bent, twisted, and distorted by other emotions and agendas.

If I have something very difficult to say to two people and one feels a bit beaten up by me and the other person knows that I love him, which one is predisposed to listen to and consider what I have to say? The answer is obvious, isn't it? If you are a child of God with a Bible in your hands, you don't need a special manual to tell you how to interact, react, and respond on social media. The gospel is your guide and Ephesians 4 is your manual. But here is the problem. As long as sin remains in us, self-centeredness will continue to be a huge temptation and selfless, other-centered living will be a bit counterintuitive. So, we should all start by confessing that we don't always care about the unity of the Spirit. Sometimes we just want to be affirmed or defend ourselves or protect our tribe or win the day. Sometimes we lack humble gentleness. Often we are driven, angry, and impatient. Sometimes we don't prize peace. And often we fail to speak the truth in love. No wonder we are such a distressed and divided community. And as you confess, cry out for the grace that is yours in Christ. Pray for rescue; no, not from the people who you think are deeply wrong or who draw out your anger. Pray that by grace you would be rescued from yourself, that is, from the selfish tendencies that still live within your heart. And then remember Ephesians 4 every time you go to Facebook, Twitter, Instagram, or TikTok. God is honored and good things happen when his children live together and communicate together with a humble commitment to protect the amazing bond between us that he alone created.

9

Limits

HUMILITY IS MORE PERSUASIVE than pride. Patience is more powerful than irritated impatience. A gentle answer is more transformative than loud and angry reactions. A willingness to listen does more good than the demand to be heard. Forgiveness is more powerful than bitterness. Love produces an infinitely better harvest than hate. Peacemaking does more good than warmongering. Mercy triumphs over judgment.

The Bible is clear that there are things you can do to function as one of God's tools of change. You can behave in ways that garner opportunities to be heard. If you believe that there is such a thing as God, that he has given us such a thing as truth, that there are such things as the forces of evil and falsehood, then you should want people to know what is true and what is false. You should care about your community and your culture and what it believes. You should care about the hearts, souls, and lives around you. You should not retreat into your safe little Christian cocoon, with your small circle of echo chamber friends. You should be involved in the world around you, and you should be involved in the unending conversation that God intends to mature and purify his church. In the Bible, opting out is nowhere presented as an option.

Yes, you should be involved with the character and commitments that Scripture calls you to, but what I am about to say next is very important. In all of your activism, as a child of God you need to quickly and humbly admit your limits. (You and I have the power to change the heart of no one.) If you could change the heart of another person by the sheer power of your logic, or skill with words, or stubborn persistence, or force of your personality, or fearfulness of your threats, or power of your position, or size of your influence, then the life, death, and resurrection of Jesus and the indwelling presence of the Spirit would not have been necessary. You and I are never the creators of change. We are only ever instruments in the hands of the one who alone has the power to create the only kind of human change that lasts—change of heart. If you forget or deny your limits, you will end up doing and saying things you should not do or say and, in so doing, fail to create the change you had in mind. Assigning to yourself the power and control over other people that only God has never results in anything good. The more I examine social media, the more I am convinced that much of the toxic insanity that lives there is the fruit of people denying or forgetting their limits.

If you want to rise above the toxic reactivity that is so harmful to the conversations of the surrounding culture and the Christian community, you have to start by humbly admitting your limits. We all tend to forget our limits and proudly try to do what only God can do. Perhaps as a parent you've fallen into thinking that raising the volume of your voice can change one of your children's hearts. Maybe your forgetfulness causes you to be comfortable with proudly destroying the logic of someone you're trying to win. Or perhaps you're tempted to buy someone's loyalty or rein someone in by a threat. In each of these examples, you have assigned yourself the ability to do what only God can do, that is, change the content and character of another person's heart. It never produces, in any lasting way, what we hoped it would produce.

It is vital that all of our reactions, interactions, and responses to one another are shaped by a humble confession of our limits. I think if we all were to do this, much of the toxic reactivity that stains the Christian conversation would be gone. So, permit me to define what I mean by our limits by running through the catalog of limits all of us have and will continue to have until we are in the forever that is on the other side.

Limited Righteousness

Having a perspective informed by the gospel is incredibly helpful here. Yes, we have been declared perfectly righteous because of the righteous life and acceptable sacrifice of Jesus Christ on our behalf. We positionally stand before God as righteous, but we are not actually perfectly righteous. We are *in the process* of becoming actually righteous. By the power of God's sanctifying grace, we are all in process. This means that sin still remains, with its moral impurity and its tendency to rebel. We don't always think in godly ways. We don't always desire what God desires for us. Our motives are often a mix of what is pure and what is impure. We are still capable of pride, hatred, and greed. There are moments when sin seems more attractive to us than obedience. We suffer from pockets of spiritual blindness and the inaccuracy of self-understanding that results. This means the war for the rulership of our hearts still goes on.

So, our spontaneous impulses will not always be right. The desires that direct what our fingers do on the keypad will not always be pure. We will be tempted to use words as weapons rather than as tools of grace. We will have times when we will be quick to speak but rather slow to listen. We will be capable of being seduced into thinking that judgment is better, when mercy is what is needed. We will be tempted to point out in others what we have tolerated in ourselves. We will be tempted to find greater joy in a takedown than in a loving moment of rescue. We will be tempted to look at those who disagree with us as enemies rather than members of our family. We will be tempted to assume we are right, while we judge the insights and motives of others. We will be tempted to personalize what is not personal and to respond out of personal hurt. As long as sin lives inside of us, we are all susceptible to these temptations, so reminding yourself that you have not arrived, that you have not graduated from God's school of grace, and that you still need his forgiving, rescuing, and empowering mercies is very important. May every reaction be shaped by a confession of limited righteousness.

Limited Knowledge

I have just been through a year-long experience of limited knowledge. Throughout the last year I wrote a book about twelve core gospel doctrines.[1] My focus was not just to define and explain these wonderful truths but to delineate how they are meant to shape everything we do and say. This project proved to be a deeply humbling experience. First I was confronted by how much easier it is for me to teach these truths than it is for me to live them. But one particular thing confronted me again and again and caused me to cry out for help again and again. I came to see how much I

---

1 *Do You Believe? 12 Historic Doctrines to Change Your Everyday Life* (Wheaton, IL: Crossway, 2021).

didn't know about what I know. God's truth is a bottomless ocean of glory. You and I can swim deeper and deeper for the rest of our lives and never come close to reaching the bottom. In fact, we will dive into the oceanic glory of God's truth for all eternity and never reach the bottom. So, we all need to humbly abandon our prideful theological-always-rightism and willingly confess that we do not know everything. We need to be willing to interact with one another with the heart of a student, always willing to learn new things or sharpen our understanding of what we already know. There are too many theological know-it-alls on Christian social media, trolling the sites looking to parade their doctrinal prowess by mockingly correcting the theological observations of a brother or sister in Christ. These are not sweet pleas made out of love for God's truth; these are prideful takedowns made out of love for self.

But we need to consider something else here. Being an expert in one area of thought or endeavor does not mean you're an expert in all. If you're a pastor, a ministry leader, or a serious Bible student, you may have come to a place of theological expertise, but it's vital to remind yourself of the limits of that expertise. You probably shouldn't be pontificating about epidemiology, social theories, political philosophy, science, medicine, or other fields outside of your particular area of knowledge and experience. We all need experts in our lives. No one is the overarching expert on everything. It is painful to watch brothers and sisters, some of them people of influence, speaking authoritatively about topics of which they have no training and little expertise. It's tempting to think you know more than you know, and it's tempting to react in ways that are less than helpful to people who you think don't know what you think *you* know. Much of the toxic reactivity we encounter would go away if we would confess that we must be committed to a student way of living and if we would remind ourselves to stay in our lane of training and expertise. Humbly admit the limits of your knowledge and the narrow focus of your expertise every time you are tempted to post an opinion or interact with the opinions of others.

Limited Experience

My dear wife, Luella, and I have had a transformative experience over the last several years. It has been one of those experiences that confronts you with how big God's world is and how limited your experience of that world is. We didn't need to travel across the world to be faced with the limits of our life experience. We only needed to travel a few miles from our home in Center City Philadelphia. We began to attend a church that has a Black pastor and about 80 percent Black attenders/members. It has been a wonderful eye-opening and heart-humbling experience. If you deny the limits of your experience, you will tend to assume your experience is everyone's experience, and because you make this assumption you don't ask, investigate, or learn about how different another person's experience is from yours. All kinds of misunderstanding and hurt result when I assume that you and I share experiences when we do not. As Luella and I listened to the experiences of our Black brothers and sisters, as we invited them to tell their stories, and as we allowed our assumptions to be confronted, we realized how wrong so many of our assumptions had been.

Yes, there is so much human stuff that we all share and so much gospel stuff that all Christians celebrate together. But growing up as a White boy in Toledo, Ohio, and growing up as a Black boy in inner city Philadelphia are simply not the same. I was confronted again and again with how wrong my assumptions had been and came to regret many of the judgmental things I had thought or said over the years that assumed a similarity of experience. We need to be better at entering the world of others with a humble heart that loves others enough to want to listen with a hunger to know and understand. We need to value the stories of others because we believe in and worship the one who is the author of those stories. So much of the toxic reactivity of social media is fueled by a prideful assumption of similarity of experience and defensive responses to people who say their experience has been vastly different from ours. Pastor, the women in your church do not have the same experience of your church that you have or even that the other men have. You should be willing to listen to the experiences of women in your church. Moms, your children do not have the same experience of your family that you and your husband have. It's important to make safe places for your children to candidly talk about life in your family. Boss, your workers do not have the same experience of your company that you have. Financially secure people do not experience life the same way the poor do. Sick people experience life very differently from those who are strong and healthy. Before you react, how about lovingly asking yourself, "Who is this person that I'm reacting to, what has her life been like, and what is going on in and around her right now?"

Limited Wisdom

I am in the process of doing a series of weekly five-minute videos on Proverbs. In each video I summarize one of the many wisdom themes that are developed in this amazing portion of God's word. I have been blown away by the depth and glory of the wisdom of God's wisdom. And it has ignited in me a deeper passion for being truly and functionally wise than I have ever had before. The Bible has so much to say about wisdom, not only what wisdom is but also how wisdom lives. People tend to confuse knowledge with wisdom. I was a seminary professor for twenty years. By the time my students got to my classroom, they had acquired tons of knowledge, but few of them were truly wise. How do I know this? When I would ask them to apply their body of knowledge to specific situations through the means of a case study, most often they couldn't do it. They had no trouble passing doctrinal exams, but applying those doctrines to the difficult situations of life in this fallen world was a different story.

This is what wisdom is and does. Wisdom is the ability to apply the truths of God's word with specificity to the situations, locations, and relationships of daily life. Knowledge is a way of thinking. Wisdom is a way of living. Knowledge meditates on what is true. Wisdom decides what is right to do. Knowledge is a commitment of the heart and mind to a body of truths. Wisdom is a commitment of everything you are and have to a way of living. Knowledge surrenders your conceptual abilities to the revelation of God. Wisdom surrenders your life to his will, his way, and his glory. Wisdom can't exist without knowledge, and knowledge is incomplete until it is applied by wisdom. Biblical knowledge was never meant to be an end in itself but a means to an end, and that end is wise, godly living. Wisdom understands that every insight, every command, every truth, every principle, every doctrine, and every promise of Scripture carries with it a culture for our everyday living. Wisdom understands that you do not know what you know until you can live what you know.

Now here's what's important about the acquisition of wisdom. Becoming wise is never an event but rather a lifelong process. We all need to be humbly willing to admit that when it comes to wisdom, we are all in a constant state of becoming. Praise God that

I am wiser than I once was and thank God that I will one day be wiser than I am now. You and I will never journey to the furthest boundaries of the wisdom of God, no matter how long we walk with him. And the fact that I am still in the process of becoming wise means that I am still capable of being a fool. Again and again, as I look at social media sites, I read the comments of people who assume that they are quite wise, while at that very moment they are reacting in ways that are quite foolish. Wisdom is humble, wisdom is kind, wisdom answers softly, wisdom is patient, wisdom is understanding, wisdom is generous, wisdom is forgiving, wisdom is just, wisdom loves mercy more than judgment, wisdom values character and God's honor over winning the day, wisdom doesn't hunt for enemies but makes many friends, and wisdom never flaunts its wisdom.

Admitting that you are not yet wise all of the time and in every way and confessing that you are still capable of acting the fool before you react is a habit many of us need. The toxic reactivity that we seem to encounter every day is driven by faux wisdom. It is a pride of knowledge coupled with a skill in communication that masquerades as wisdom; but it does not do what wisdom would or produce what wisdom could. It often claims to defend God's truth, but in a way that does not give him honor. It claims to love God, but treats brothers and sisters as enemies. Wisdom that lacks patient humility and forgiving love is a form of "wisdom" that is not wise. God graces us with his wisdom and by grace works to make us wise. We should all remember the words of Proverbs 4:7–9:

> The beginning of wisdom is this: Get wisdom,
> and whatever you get, get insight.
> Prize her highly, and she will exalt you;

she will honor you if you embrace her.
She will place on your head a graceful garland;
she will bestow on you a beautiful crown.

Live, react, respond, and pray as a wisdom-needy person. It will change how you act, react, and respond, and it will produce a harvest of good fruit.

Limited Gifts and Abilities

In my ministry I have been confronted with the limits of my gifts. I am thankful for the gifts God has given me, but I am aware that I am not gifted in every way or for everything. I have been gifted by God to teach, preach, counsel, and write, but I am not an administrator. So I have surrounded myself with people who are smarter than me, and I try to tell them again and again how much I value, respect, and appreciate each one of them. I could not do what God has called me to do without their work, advice, counsel, and direction. This is how God meant it to be. None of us has been designed to function independently. Each of our lives is a community project. Each of us is dependent on the contribution of others in order to be what we're supposed to be and do what we've been called to do. The word picture that the apostle Paul uses for this is the physical body (1 Cor. 12). Each part of the body is dependent on every other part of the body. Each part must do its part for each part to be able to do its part. No part of the body functions properly in isolation. This means that a humble admission of the limits of gifts and a humble dependency on and thankfulness for the gifts of others are prerequisite if the body of Christ is ever going to function as God intended.

If you believe in divinely intended interdependency, then you don't burn relationships to make a point. You don't turn into enemies people who are not your enemies. You don't publicly mock someone you should respect. You don't divide into adversarial tribes. You don't dismiss the contributions of others. You never do anything with the intention of harm. You won't be quick to question a person's character or judge his motives. You won't value digital followers more than friends. If you embrace the limits of your gifts and the need you have for others, then you will treat others, personally or online, with respect, appreciation, thankfulness, and love. You will be quick to listen and slow to react. You will disagree in a way that strengthens relationships. You will invite people in and receive their contributions with gratitude. None of us have it all and all of us need one another. The conversation on social media would be radically different if we all believed this and responded to one another as if we did.

Limited Time

When Steve Jobs made mobile screens ubiquitous, the entire culture of the world changed. We now carry in our purses and pockets a tool so incredibly powerful that forty years ago the thought of such a thing would have been seen as science fiction. With our mobile devices came the internet, and with it came Google, email, Facebook, Instagram, TikTok, Twitter, and tens of thousands of apps that command our time and attention. We go nowhere without these powerful and seductive devices. They greet us in the morning and they put us to sleep at night. They are a constant distraction, interrupting everything we do. Our mobile devices are powerful instruments for good, but they control us too much. Incessant mobile connectivity tricks us into thinking that we need what we don't actually need and that we have to do things that we really don't have to do. Nothing has changed human culture more dramatically in the last decade than these devices. All of our lives have been reshaped by their power.

Here's why this is important. By God's good and wise design, you and I have only a limited amount of time. You will never get ten days in a week or thirty-two hours in a day. You and I do not have the option of living beyond the limits that God has set for us. So if something comes into your life that is powerful, attractive, and seductive and eats up a lot of your time, the time will be taken from something else in your life. If your job takes more and more of your time, then it will eat into your family time, your friendships and fellowship time, or your ministry time. This is true of our powerful media devices and the social media sites that seem to magnetize and captivate us. The hours we spend scrolling take time away from our wives, our children, our devotional time, our time with brothers and sisters in Christ, and on and on. When it comes to the huge amount of hours spent on social media, time invested is time stolen. I am persuaded we get sucked into the toxicity that is around us because digital culture has become too valuable to us. In those moments when we could be investing in the various things God has called us to, we are thinking about things we don't need to think about and being tempted to respond in ways that we should not. May the presence of your phone with you all the time be a physical warning of the limits of your time. May we all learn to say no and renew our commitment to invest in things that God says have lasting value.

We all live with a variety of limits that God, in his wisdom, goodness, and love, has set for us. It never is a good thing to attempt to live beyond those limits. With peace of heart we can stay inside of those limits because we know the one who has set them for us and we know that all of his ways are right and true. The boundaries he has set for us are protective boundaries. They keep us from being tempted to try to do what only he can do or to say things that we should not say. It is important to remember that God is constantly doing for us, through us, and in us what we are too limited to do for ourselves or others. So before you post a reaction or text a response, stop and remember the limits of your righteousness, knowledge, experience, wisdom, gifts, and time. In the end, you will thank God that you did.

10

Values

YOU AND I DO IT EVERY DAY. In fact, we do it a hundred times a day. It is inescapable because we were designed to do it. What we desire, what we choose, what we decide, how we react, what we place our hopes and dreams on, what we commit ourselves to, where we feel disappointment and anger, where we persevere, and when we quit are all determined by this. It causes us to be divided and it makes us assemble into tribes. It causes us to idolize some people and pity others. Every day, in more ways than we tend to be aware of, *we assign value to things*. Every day we act, react, and respond based on what we think is important and what we have decided is not. We are all value-oriented, purpose-oriented, importance-oriented, goal-oriented human beings. Everything we do and say, we do and say in pursuit of what is valuable to us. Between the "already" and the "not yet" we all live with a values struggle. Different value systems tempt and tug at us. And we will never understand the importance and struggles of values until we understand that this is not just a battle of competing value systems but a struggle of worship.

I am blown away by the depth of insight found in the pages of God's word and how radically different its analysis of the problems of life is. We find nothing like it anywhere else. The Bible offers us a deep and penetrating analysis of human beings and why they do the things they do. Its analysis is far from being simple; it is layered and able to deal with the complexities of human motivation and behavior. We would do well not to abandon the diagnostic splendor of Scripture for other analyses that fail to get at the heart of our dysfunction. When it comes to our personal operational systems of value, the Bible has a lot to offer. And this topic is important for this book because underneath toxic reactivity are deeply held, thought-engaging, and reaction-shaping values.

Worship and Values

The values that drive the way we react are not so much rooted in instilled family values or cultural values systems, although they are very influential, but in something deeper and more determinative: worship. This statement requires definition and explanation. So what is worship? When most people think of worship, they think of formal, visible, gathered religion. They think of a Sunday morning service with all its familiar traditions. But a vast percentage of our worship takes place outside of Sunday morning formal worship. The worship that actually shapes and directs your life is informal, often unnoticed, and takes place in the regular spaces, activities, and relationships of your daily life. Whether you know it or not, you never stop worshiping. The most self-consciously religious person and the most avowedly irreligious person share one thing in common: they both worship every day in places where they might never think that worship exists.

To understand how this can be, you have to understand that worship is not just an activity that some people give themselves to. No, worship is a fundamental *identity* that all people share. To be human means you are a worshiping being. Your heart, being the control center of your personhood, was designed by God to be a worship center. In others words, our hearts are always being ruled by something. You and I are always living for something. We are always living in pursuit of something that we think will deliver life (however we define it) to us. Jesus captures this worship dynamic with the word *treasure* (Matt. 6:19–21). A treasure is something of value that is worth seeking, possessing, enjoying, and celebrating. Embedded in Christ's teaching are three "treasure principles":

1. Everyone lives for some kind of treasure.
2. The thing that is your treasure will control your heart.
3. What controls your heart will control your words and behavior.

You may be wondering what this has to do with the socially dysfunctional mess that social media has become. Here it is. You will never fully understand that mess until you understand that it is driven by treasure. Certain values drive the toxicity that darkens our digital conversation every day. Whether they know it or not, people post in pursuit of treasure because that's who human beings are and that's what human beings do. You could argue that everything we do and everything we say, we do and say in pursuit of some kind of treasure. If you're arguing your friend into a humiliating corner, you are doing so because winning is a more valuable treasure to you at that point than relationship. If you're working so much that you have become an absentee father and husband, then it may be that material success is a more valuable treasure to you than family. If you are scanning porn sites on your work computer, then sexual pleasure is more valuable to you than being a trustworthy and faithful employee. If you are eating your way into obesity and poor health, then the pleasure of food is a more valuable treasure to you than your physical well-being. And if you troll people on social media, then the clickbait takedown has become a more valuable treasure to you than gentle, patient, kind, and merciful love.

The Bible makes it clear that there are only two categories of treasure. Jesus says that your heart is captivated by either treasure on earth or treasure in heaven (Matt. 6). The apostle Paul says that you are either worshiping the Creator or worshiping the creation (Rom. 1). Everything we do or say is shaped, driven, and directed by one of these. God designed our worship orientation to drive us to him in love, service, joyful submission, and satisfaction of heart. Sin causes us to turn from God and give our hearts in love, service, and submission to an endless catalog of God-replacements, asking the created thing to give us the contentment of heart that only God can give. This means that everything you say or post is shaped by a heart that is ruled either by God or by something in the creation. You and I always say what we say and do what we do in pursuit of something.

Let me give you the bottom line and then explain it. *If we have worshiped our way into this toxic mess, then to solve it we will have to worship our way out.* What you do, what you say, how you see your world, how you assess situations and people, what you think is right and wrong, how you respond when feeling wronged, how you make choices and decisions, and how you evaluate how you've acted and reacted are all shaped and controlled by what you worship. Whatever has control of your heart, whatever is most important to you, whatever you've determined you can't live without, that is, whatever you worship will always be exposed by how you conduct yourself on social media or in your everyday relationships at home, work, church, and in the public arena. So, if you are a regular part of the toxic reactivity that has stained these arenas, the way out is not some new set of social-media or personal-relationship rules. The way out is not reaction management; no, it's worship realignment.

Perhaps the Christian social media landscape is what it now is because *we don't love God as much as we say we do*. Perhaps the way we react and respond to one another exposes the reality that we don't actually love what God loves or value what he values. Perhaps what we want, what we think we deserve, or what we think someone else deserves is more important to us than God's holy call and honor. Perhaps, at street level, our allegiance is to another kingdom rather than his kingdom of righteousness, truth, and love. Perhaps we want to be king rather than loyal servants of the King.

You see, the meanness, rapid judgment, character assassination, cruelty, vengeance, and dismissal that lives on Christian social media is not first about breaking God's rules; it's about breaking relationship with the one who created these rules for us. Consider the Ten Commandments. You will keep God's commands, you will value what he values, and you will love as he loves only when love for him and a desire for his honor is what effectively and functionally rules your heart. Your values are always formed by what you worship. Your choices are always shaped by what you worship. Your behavior is always directed by what you worship. Your words, digital or audible, are always controlled by what you worship. The culture of reactivity is a relationship/worship problem, and confessing this is the only way lasting change will ever take place.

Let me give you one example of what it would look like if God were in his rightful place in our hearts, so that we valued what he values. Consider with me Galatians 5:22–26:

> But the fruit of the Spirit is love, joy, peace, patience, kindness, goodness, faithfulness, gentleness, self-control; against such things there is no law. And those who belong to Christ Jesus have crucified the flesh with its passions and desires.
>
> If we live by the Spirit, let us also keep in step with the Spirit. Let us not become conceited, provoking one another, envying one another.

This passage is a brilliant, clear, insightful, and transformative example of what God values. The passage begins with the word *but* because Paul is making a contrast between the fruit of the Spirit and the works of the flesh. As I stated earlier, he calls these character qualities fruit of the Spirit because they are only possible for us because of the power of the Holy Spirit living within us. Jesus lived as we could not live, died in our place, and rose victorious over sin and death so that you and I would not only have eternal life but also a new identity and new potential. That potential is made possible by the gift of the Spirit, who convicts of sin and empowers us to live in a brand-new way. God values the things in this passage so much that he was willing to make the most valuable and costly of sacrifices, the sacrifice of his Son, so that we could have these things in our lives. This means:

God values love.
God values joy.
God values patience.

God values kindness.
God values goodness.
God values faithfulness.
God values gentleness.
God values self-control.

The central question of this book is: In the situations, relation-ships, and social media interactions of our daily lives, do we? Is God so in control of the thoughts, desires, and motivations of our hearts that we value what he values, we love what he loves, and we want what he wants? What would it look like if every word that came out of us, personal or digital, were formed by us valu-ing what God values? How many things would we never post or say? How different would our reactions be to those who disagree with us? How different would our responses be to those who we feel have wronged us? How different would our defense of the truth be? How different would our responses be to those who we think are enemies of what is right, good, and true? How different would our responses be to people of different races, ethnicities, cultures, social class, position, or gender? How different would our goal for our words be? Here is the point. When you really do value what God values, by grace you are being rescued from you. You are being protected from all the dark reactive instincts that are the result of remaining sin. And when you are being rescued from you, you respond to others in brand-new, beautiful, and God-honoring ways.

This is why Paul concludes this passage the way he does. If you value what the Holy Spirit is working to produce in you and through you, then you will keep in step with him, that is, you will go, in all of your relationships, where he is going. This means:

- You won't be conceited (putting yourself in the center, making it all about you).
- You won't provoke (inciting others because you love being in the middle of the fight).
- You won't envy (enjoying taking down those who have what you think you deserve).

The larger context of the passage is freedom, the freedom that only the grace of the gospel can ever give you. Grace frees you from your bondage to the idolatry, impurity, enmity, strife, jealousy, fits of anger, rivalries, divisions, and envy of your former life. And grace not only frees you to live in a brand-new and much more beautiful way, but it also empowers you to do so. If this is so, then why would we not want to go where the Spirit is going? The only answer is because we don't value what God values, because other things have replaced him in our hearts. Humbly confessing our functional idolatry is the first step in the change that is so desperately needed not just in the surrounding culture but in the Christian community as well. As we confess, we must remember that our problem is not just the control of evil desires in our hearts. The desire for even a good thing can become a bad thing if it becomes a ruling thing. It is good to want some control in your life, but if your heart is ruled by control, you will destroy your life and relationships. It's good to want to be happy, but if happiness rules you, you will be endlessly demanding, frustrated, and angry. It's good to want to know right and be right, but if being right rules you, you will be critical, unapproachable, judgmental, and unlivable. It's good to want relationships, but if your heart is ruled by the acceptance of others, you will be entitled and demanding or paralyzed by fear of man. There is no other safe lord over your heart than the Lord of lords. And there is no better way of living than to value what he values.

I want to propose six street-level examples of what it means in our current cultural climate to value what God values.

Values That Counter a Reactive Culture

The gospel is of greater value than politics. If you are a believer in the Lord Jesus Christ, politics should not form your foundational worldview; the gospel should. If you are a believer, politics is not what should give you your identity; the gospel should. If you are a believer, political power should not give you hope; the gospel should. If you are a believer, you should give your life not to any earthly king but to the King of kings. In this moment, politics and political power have become too important, too central, and too life-shaping; they have become a seedbed of much division, acrimony, and reactivity in the Christian community.

Relationships are of greater value than dominating the conversation and winning the day. The gospel is entirely relational. Christ purchased for us peace with God and, through that peace, peace with one another. The gospel teaches us that our walk with God is not an individual pursuit but a community project. Second only to the command to love God above all else is the command to love your neighbor as yourself. The problem is that so much of our contact with one another, so much of our ongoing conversation, and so much of our debate of the issues of the day are no longer personal but digital. In this arena, people become dehumanized; they become post, clicks, or likes. Because we lose the sense of flesh-and-blood relationships that necessitate commitment and carry consequences, we allow ourselves to behave on social media in ways that are antisocial, not recognizing the value of our relationships with one another.

God's honor is of greater value than your comfort, appreciation, and respect. So much of the toxic reactivity that greets us every day is the result of a self-focused, self-aggrandizing, and self-referencing way of looking at and experiencing the world. It is me in the center, and the offenses that grieve, anger, and motivate me the most are perceived offenses against *me.* It is an entitled and demanding way of living that never produces personal happiness or relational peace. The gospel of Jesus Christ is meant to produce in you a heart-shaping awe of God that makes his glory the thing that then directs everything you do and say. Self-glory always destroys community and is a sad substitute for the true peace and happiness that is to be found in living for the glory of one infinitely greater than you.

Unity is of greater value than individualism or tribalism. Sadly, sin causes us to be better at division than unity. Sin causes us to confuse unity with a demand for uniformity. Sin causes us to think that we can do individually what can only be accomplished in community with others. Sin causes us to divide into little issue/theology/affinity tribes, often treating those outside of our tribe as if they were the enemy. The very nature of social media is that it makes it all too easy to succumb to these temptations. Perhaps the evangelical church has never been more divided and more at war with itself than it is right now. In Jesus's final prayer, he argues for the value of our unity with one another (see John 17). He argues that our unity with one another is meant to be a powerful argument for the gospel. You cannot read Scripture without concluding that this unity is not a luxury but essential for our continuing growth in grace and our ongoing witness to the world.

Love is of greater value than even the most subtle forms of hate.
More than once people have reacted to something I tweeted with
accusatory, character-judging, and dismissive responses. These kinds
of responses do not come from a heart of love. They do not lovingly
encourage me to reflect, reconsider, or repent. They are the words
of judgment and dismissal. Sadly, they are posted by brothers and
sisters in Christ, who are bound together with me in a unity that
only the Holy Spirit can create. Together we are to be known for
our love for one another. The subtle hatred of disrespect, dismissal,
mockery, cancellation, and judgment never produces good fruit.
When someone yells at you, you defend yourself; you don't open
up your heart. Only love has the power to break down my defenses,
creating a safe place for me to take an honest look at myself. And
love assures me that you are for me and will be with me even when
sin and disagreement get in the way.

Character is of greater value than position or power. One functional
idol in the current Christian culture is power. For the purpose of
political power, we will compromise our character and close our eyes
to the character flaws of the leaders we've attached our hopes to.
In his word God listed the qualifications for leaders in his church.
The entire list is a character list, with the exception of one skill set
(the ability to teach). God's call to every believer is "Be holy as I
am holy." Holiness forever trumps power. Holiness forever trumps
position. Holiness is not only God's call; it is what his grace works
to produce in us every day. There are too many Christian bullies
on social media. There are too many bully leaders in the church.
No Christian community can remain healthy if the quest for power
and position motivates us more than the beauty of godliness.

*

This chapter was a hard and convicting one to write. Writing it has reminded me that I am a man in constant need of Scripture's values-clarification. Things can rise in value in my heart way above their true value and, when they do, for that moment they replace my Lord and his call as the functional motivators of what I do and say. You can't examine the toxic reactivity that is so harmful to the church and to our witness to the world without concluding that we have a values problem, and that means we have a worship problem. But we can talk candidly about these things because the grace of Christ frees us from hiding and denying. There is no sin, weakness, or failure that hasn't been covered in the life, death, and resurrection of Jesus. Because of this we can look at hard subjects with hope, courage, honesty, and humility, assured that when we do, we are greeted with both forgiving and empowering grace. May we examine the worship of our hearts and the values by which we live, confessing where needed and committing ourselves to strive to keep important in our hearts what God has said is important.

11

Dignity

AS THE CRESCENDO ACT OF CREATION, God dips his hand in the dust on the ground and breathes into it, and from nothing Adam becomes a living, breathing, and fully functioning human being. With the exception of the incarnation, crucifixion, and resurrection of Jesus, there is no more wonderful, mysterious, important, and glorious moment in history. Reading the account in Genesis should stop you in your tracks and take your breath away. It should fill you with wonder and awe. It should send you to your knees in worship and adoration. And it should change the way you think about yourself and every other human being that has, is, and will populate this little ball we call Earth.

I live in Center City Philadelphia, so I walk everywhere. Of course, I don't walk the streets of my city alone. I am on the sidewalk every day with men, women, boys, and girls, and when I am, I often think of that moment when God breathed humanity into humanity. I am constantly blown away by the majesty and anatomical, physiological, emotional, psychological, intellectual, and spiritual complexity and diversity of human beings. People are a wonder. We all need to stop once in a while and take in the wonder. Consider for a moment:

- How various systems of a newborn's body all turn on at the moment of birth.
- How a little child begins to understand and form language.
- How each child is differently interested and gifted.
- The ability people have to learn a wide variety of things and apply them to life.
- The ability we all have to craft, create, and design.
- A composer's ability to create a soundscape that takes you to a different world.
- The ability of the eyes and hands of an artist to put beauty on canvas.
- The skill of an author to put words on a page that capture your imagination.
- The skill of a chef to manipulate food to excite your tongue.
- The gift of a teacher to communicate scientific, historical, or theological fact.
- The ability of an architect to create a beautiful, stable, and usable edifice.
- The tender touch of a nursing mother.
- The stern warning voice of a father.
- The encouraging hug of a friend.
- The collected wisdom of an old man.

I could go on and on. We need to allow ourselves to take time to be amazed at the stunning, multifaceted glory of what God created that moment when he breathed life into Adam. We can never allow ourselves to lose our wonder because if we do, we will not bow in awe to our Creator as we should and we will not respond to one another out of awe as we should. Every person is a walking wonder, an interdependent, interlocking system of wonderful things all working together, according to God's design, to live, breathe, think, emote, work, laugh, worship, and relate. There is no boring person. To be a human being is to be a magnificently created thing, more wonderful than the awesome pyramid, the highest peak, the expansive ocean, the glorious sunset, the powerful storm, the grand piece of music, or the most stunning painting. On the mountain peak of creation dust was turned into something alive and glorious, a person. The glory of this must never be lost on us.

Made in God's Image

But, yes, there is more. As he was creating the very first person, God uttered seven words that change everything you would otherwise think or know about people. He said, "Let us make man in our image" (Gen. 1:26). These words not only fill this moment with even greater glory than what I have already described, but they separate mankind from all of the rest of creation. Every created being or thing reflects the glory of God somehow, someway. (Every created thing was made to be a finger pointing to the glory of its designer and Creator.) But what is said at Adam's creation is said about nothing else God made. God said it and Moses recorded it so that we would forever acknowledge the distinctiveness and the superiority of human beings in God's created order. It is not enough to say that people reflect God's glory. We must also be careful to say again and again, to ourselves and to one another, that we are also made in his image, that is, in his likeness. Let this sink in. By means of the intentionality of God's design, human beings are more like God than they are like the rest of creation. Without those seven words, we fail to know and accurately understand ourselves or others.

Think about the expansive implications of what it would mean for the way we think about our own identity and the identity of everyone else if we were to truly believe that every human being who has ever lived is stamped forever with the image of God. There is no human junk, there are no little people, and no one is lesser. People have been chosen by God to carry a position of dignity that nothing else in creation has. Consider the words of Psalm 8:

> When I look at your heavens, the work of your fingers,
> > the moon and the stars, which you have set in place,
> what is man that you are mindful of him,
> > and the son of man that you care for him?
> Yet you have made him a little lower than the heavenly beings
> > and crowned him with glory and honor.
> You have given him dominion over the works of your hands;
> > you have put all things under his feet,
> all sheep and oxen,
> > and also the beasts of the field,
> the birds of the heavens, and the fish of the sea,
> > whatever passes along the paths of the seas. (Ps. 8:3–8)

I love the context of the question "What is man that you are mindful of him?" In comparison to the expansive grandeur of the heavens and the shining glory of the moon and stars, how do little insignificant people get any of God's attention? The psalm gives the resounding answer, one we must never let ourselves forget. Man is unique in the economy of God's creation because:

God made him a little lower than the angels.

God crowned him with glory and honor.

God gave him dominion over the works of his hands.

God put all things under his feet.

These four statements should stop us; they should alert us and amaze us. Here is a definition of who God designed every human being to be. This is the position and identity he created for each of us. The lofty, godlike dignity of every human being is not up for discussion, assessment, or vote. The decision was made by the Creator and communicated in seven clear words: ("Let us make man in our image,")and further defined by him in four statements in Psalm 8. With this identity comes a calling: we are to treat one another with the dignity that God placed on each one of us as his image bearers. This means I am to treat you with dignity not because of your beauty, your race, your achievements, your money, your power, your position, your family, your education, your location, your possessions, your morality, your theology, your sexuality, your spirituality, your gender, your maturity, your emotional stability, your intellectual ability, your physical strength, or your gifts and abilities, but because you bear God's likeness.

I should look into the face of any human being and see the likeness of God. I live in a densely populated center of a big city. I see more pavement than green. But I don't need to travel out to the country outside of Philadelphia to have creation remind me of the presence and glory of God. All I have to do is leave my loft, and I see his glory again and again as I pass by his image bearers on the street. I am blessed to be surrounded every day by his likeness and reminded of his presence and glory. I think in physical, face-to-face personal relationships it is easy for us to forget who we're looking at and, in God's plan, what every human being represents. And when we forget, we treat people as less than image bearers. We get mad when a person is in our way, as if he's more of an object than a person. We treat people as problems to be solved, not as those who bear God's likeness. We see people as vehicles of our success and not those who bear God's image. We separate ourselves from people because they are different and, in so doing, deny the dignity that we share. We let race, gender, social class, political views, religion, and a host of other things determine who we think people are and how they should be treated. When we forget the seven words spoken at creation, we will fail to treat people with honor and dignity, no matter what.

The world of the internet and social media makes what we are discussing here all the more difficult. In this world people are nonphysical, faceless, and often nameless. People become Twitter handles, posts, clicks, or electronic letters on a screen. People get reduced to their last comment or post. They are shrunken down to ideas we love or hate. They bear the likeness of a theology, a political position, a product, a worldview, or a tribe, but not the image of God. In this digital world, I don't see you, I don't know you, and I don't share space with you. I am afraid that with the domination of the internet and social media over our communication and much of our connection with one another, we lose our humanity. When God breathed humanity into humanity, he at the same time crowned human beings with glory and honor by saying, "This one is made in my likeness." When I am counting views, likes, comments, and retweets, people have quit being people to me. They are numbers that communicate some kind of value to me, but they have lost their humanity. And because they have, social media has become one big dignity black hole, where we give ourselves permission to treat one another in ways that most of us probably wouldn't think of doing if we were standing face-to-face with the person and seeing in their face the face of God.

Most people don't tend to go to social media to love their neighbors as themselves or to give grace to a person who desperately needs grace. Most people don't go to Twitter to comfort, encourage, and instill hope. Most of us don't go to our favorite sites to look for the latest acts of gentleness and kindness. The trending topics on social media don't tend to be about human dignity, love, mercy, justice, or forgiveness. Hours on social media won't tend to lift you up or cause you to be better prepared to treat your neighbor with dignity and love. Social media won't tend to ignite and motivate your respect and appreciation of others. Sadly, social media tends to distort relationships and plunder our humanity. It is a place where Francis Schaeffer's words, "man's inhumanity to man," seem to daily come true.[1] And I have to say, once again, that this is not just true of the surrounding culture but it is true of the Christian community as well. It's so easy for charges, accusations, judgments, threats, slanders, dismissals, and mockery to fly off our fingers and onto our screens, with little thought to whom we are reacting and the damage our words may do. For us who believe in a literal creation, dignity is not just a creational declaration but it is also a moral relational mandate.

We, of all communities, have the insight and mandate to use these powerful tools in a very different manner. I have determined to remember that everyone who reads my social media posts is a person made in the image of God. I have committed myself to use these powerful tools as tools of love and truth, and of rescuing,

---

1   Francis Schaeffer, *The God Who Is There*, in *The Francis Schaeffer Trilogy* (Wheaton, IL: Crossway, 1990), 118.

restoring, and healing grace. When I sit at my screen, I try to envision real people sitting in front of me so I will remember to post in a way that is filled with dignity and love. I have determined to stay out of the Twitter muck, to not rise quickly to my own defense, to stay true to my gospel calling, to resist reducing people to positions, ideas, or tribes, and with every touch of a key to love my neighbor as myself. I have determined to read and reflect way more than I respond and to never quickly react. I have restricted myself to posting the gospel of God's grace to protect myself from the temptation to use these powerful tools in ways they should not be used. Some of you are models of the good that can be done through these powerful media tools, and I am convinced that all of us can do better. When it comes to social media, we should be that city on a hill, a light for all to see, showing the glorious good that can be done through this amazing media. But a whole lot of confessing and repenting is necessary to get us there.

Before we look at what it means to always treat everyone with dignity, I want to make a clarification. I am not calling here for a Hallmark card approach to social media, where we put on a happy face and deny the daily struggles of life in a fallen world. I surely am not saying that we should project faux joy to protect Jesus's reputation. Life in a fallen world is difficult. Many of us are suffering, and we need to be honest about the trials of life. There are destructive lies to be exposed. The church fails, and where it does, it needs to be examined and lessons drawn from its failures. There are crucially important debates that we need to have. There is a place for righteous anger with evil. There is darkness that needs to be exposed and people who need to be confronted. The Bible never asks us to put on a happy face, spewing quasi-spiritual cliches while denying reality. Biblical faith never requires that we minimize, ignore, or deny the things we face in this fallen world. This chapter is not about denial but about (the way we talk to one another about the things that are necessary to discuss.) Because of who human beings are by God's design and their lofty place in God's economy, we should always treat everyone with dignity no matter who they are, no matter what they're doing, no matter what they represent, no matter how wrong and reprehensible it is to us. There simply is no exception clause to God's holy and all-encompassing command "You shall love your neighbor as yourself."

How We Treat Others with Dignity

So what does it mean to treat people with dignity? It means:

- *I will treat every person with respect, no matter what.* This is respect that does not have to be earned. It is the honor that is yours because you bear the image of God. I must be careful not to give myself permission to be disrespectful and cruel because you are the enemy of what I think is good, true, and beautiful. I respect you not because of what I think of you, but because of whom God has created and declared you to be.
- *I will intentionally do harm to no one.* Scripture clearly forbids that we would act in any way to harm our neighbor. The Bible prohibits murder, forbids any act of vengeance, calls us to be angry without sinning, and commands us not to gossip. Scripture is clear that all of our responses to one another are to be shaped and directed by love, even if that person is your enemy.
- *I will take seriously the experiences of others.* It is so easy to dehumanize the person I do not know but whose opinion

a real person I dislike. It is easy to forget that (there is a real person behind the post that has just riled me up.) It is important to remember that (behind the post, opinion, click, like, or rant is a real person with all the pressures and stressors of life) in a fallen world. I might not know what leads people to the places where they are, but I do know that (life) in this broken world (is hard and requires patience, sympathy, and understanding.)

- *I will respond to differences with appreciation and grace.* Scripture calls us to unity not to uniformity. God has made us different from one another in many ways. (He has written different stories for us, with different shaping influences.) We don't come to the same things in the same ways. We don't express the same things in the same ways. We don't see and experience the same things in the same ways. Even those of us who have submitted our hearts and lives to God's truth don't see that truth in the same way. There is such a thing as moral right and wrong, but not all our differences are a matter of moral right or wrong. (So we approach one another with humility, kindness, graciousness, appreciation, patience, and grace.)

- *I will look on others with sympathy, not apathy or antipathy.* People who seem lost to us, who are morally wrong, who are convinced that what is false is true, or who live as functional enemies of God should not draw hatred out of us but sympathy. When someone who is lost comes to you and asks for directions, you don't hate him, you don't mock him; you sympathize with his plight and you gladly give him the directions he needs. (If what I have I didn't earn but rather got by grace, shouldn't I want that same grace for the person who doesn't have it?)

- *I will require myself to remember that other people are image bearers.* We cannot do this enough. In every encounter, personal or digital, keep saying to yourself, "This person is an image bearer, this person is an imager bearer, this person is an . . ."
- *I will think of no one as beyond redemption.* We must view no one and respond to no one as if he or she is beyond the reach of God's redeeming grace. No one is a lost cause. There is no sin so great, no darkness so deep, and no rebellion so strong that it lives beyond the rescuing, convicting, forgiving, transforming, and delivering power of God's grace. We need to respond to everyone, remembering that no matter how deep the hole of darkness and sin is, God's grace is deeper.

As we close this chapter, I am reminded that the ultimate fulfillment of the words of Psalm 8 is Jesus. He is crowned with glory and honor. As the conquering Savior King, all things have been placed under his feet. And because of that, he is our help and hope. It is not natural for us to love our enemies. It is not natural for us to speak with words of grace to those who oppose what we know to be true. It's not natural for me to treat someone with respect whose lifestyle God says is immoral. Sinful anger is easier for me than righteous anger. So I am again confronted with the fact that I am a person in need of help, and I suspect that you are too. That help is ours for the asking because of who Jesus is and what he has done. Why don't you reach out for that help right here, right now? Confess your failure, receive his forgiveness, and cry out for his empowering grace.

12

Presence

FROM THE VERY BEGINNING, I saw social media as a powerful tool for gospel proclamation and encouragement. Every day I post gospel content on multiple sites and, because I do, I have a rather large following. This means I am regularly trolled, that is, mocked, accused, mischaracterized, disrespected, or dismissed. So I have committed myself to functioning on social media as if I actually believe in the presence, power, and unceasing activity of my Lord. It is a discipline I have had to commit myself to. And because I work to live out of confidence in the Lord's presence, I commit myself to follow his example.

No human being was disrespected more than Jesus. No one was more harshly questioned or rudely mocked than him. No one suffered more personal injustice than he did. No one had a greater right to rise to his own defense than Jesus did, but he didn't. He allowed nothing to distract or derail him from his re-demptive mission. He came to do his Father's will, and that was all he was ever going to do. He believed there was a greater and more powerful judgment than the judgment of his listeners or his antagonists, and he believed the Judge was perfect in every way. So he continued to declare who he was and what he had come to do, without answering every charge and taking every opportunity to rise to his own defense. Even in the face of threats he stood resolute. The presence of this one is my daily hope and comfort. His presence keeps me from losing my way, forgetting my calling, and making the mission about me.

Jesus's example gives me practical direction as the shots come my way. Peter says it like this: "When he was reviled, he did not revile in return; when he suffered, he did not threaten, but continued entrusting himself to him who judges justly" (1 Pet. 2:23). This passage has been like a protective mentor to me. In this culture of toxic reactivity, I have committed myself to follow the example of this one who is right now present with me. I have committed myself to believe in his perfectly holy justice. I believe if he can't protect the reputation of those he has called to represent him, then no one can. I will not mock in return when I am mocked. I will not threaten those who have threatened me. I will suffer with character and grace because I know whom I serve. I will remember his presence, I will start each day reminding myself of my identity as his child, I will commit myself to obey his commands and to follow his example, and I will firmly believe there is present blessing and future reward in doing so. I do all of this with peace and rest of heart because I know my Lord is holy and good. These commitments are not always easy for me. I do get angry. I do at moments wonder what my Lord is doing. I am tempted to fire back at someone who has shot at me, and I am capable of being hurt. But I have also tasted the blessing of not making the offenses against me the most motivating factors in my life. I run to this passage every day:

You keep him in perfect peace
whose mind is stayed on you,
because he trusts in you. (Isa. 26:3)

I get up every morning not striving to justify my words to my accusers but striving to trust in my Lord. The former will never result in perfect peace of heart, but the latter will give you peace, calm, and rest of heart you can find no other way.

I want to end this book thinking about what it practically means to act, react, and respond out of a deep belief in the presence, power, goodness, holiness, justice, and mercy of the Lord.

If I am resting in his presence:

- *I will always speak in a way that gives grace to the hearer (Eph. 4:29).* I can always speak words of grace because I believe in a God of grace, whose grace is the most powerful force of personal heart and life transformation in the universe. Because he exists, rules every situation I am in, empowers me to do what he has called me to do, and has the power to accomplish what I could never accomplish on my own, I don't have to force change that I have no power to create. Resting in the presence and power of the Redeemer means I don't have to try, by the power of my words, the force of my personality, the size of my anger, or whatever else, to do the work in the hearts of others that only he can do. *Do your words always give grace?*
- *I will not let the sun go down on my anger (Eph. 4:26).* When the comment line turns dark, when judgments fly or accusations abound, I am comforted by the fact that there is a righteous Judge on the throne of the universe. He will always do what is right in the face of wrong. He is the only truly holy and wise dispenser

of vengeance. It is a grace that I am able to stand aside and not get in the way of his perfectly righteous anger. He is the ultimate defender of his children and his truth. So at the end of the day, in an act of faith, I surrender my anger to him and rest in peace, knowing that my life, my ministry, and my world are in the best hands. *Do you carry your anger or submit it to him?*

• *I will submit to God's kingship, not try to build a kingdom of my own (Matt. 6:33).* My citizenship in the kingdom of God means I am freed from using my personal relationships and my social media accounts to build my own kingdom. Because I have been chosen to be an ambassador of the King, I am freed from the burden of trying to be the king. I am no longer working to build my "brand," to collect followers, to be prominent, or to wield power. I do want to be an influencer—not to drive people to me but to introduce them to my Savior King. Only when I love the King and his kingdom will I properly love others and be freed from seducing them into submitting to my kingdom intentions. I serve a victorious, present, and reigning King, and that changes everything. *In all your reactions, whose kingdom are you seeking to build?*

• *I will believe that as a child of God I have the power to resist the devil (James 4:7).* Not because I have independent spiritual insight or power, but because God is in me, with me, and for me do I have power to say no to the myriad temptations that this reactive culture puts before me every day. There are posts that make me mad, hurt me, or falsely accuse me and, when they do, it is tempting to jump into the toxic pool of reactivity and let it rip in my own defense. But I am not reliant on my own power because I serve the one who has defeated Satan. So I can resist him too. I really am able to love my enemies,

I actually can do good to those who mistreat me, and I have the power, when threatened, not to threaten in return. I can resist the temptation to respond to sin with sin, because the one who conquered sin has made me the temple where he dwells. *Are you exercising the power that is yours to resist the temptations of this reactive culture?*

• *I will commit to not think of myself more highly than I ought to think (Rom. 12:3).* Nothing is more humbling than standing before the holiness, infinite power, perfect wisdom, spotless love, and faithful grace of the King of kings. You and I will only ever see ourselves accurately when we look at ourselves through the lens of his incalculable glory. Not thinking of yourself more highly than you ought to think is much, much more than working to be humble. It is being humbled by opening your eyes to all that God is and all that you are not. You live, with open eyes and an open heart, in the shadow of the majesty of the Lord Almighty. His ever-present glory crushes the human arrogance that causes us to be more concerned about our rights, reputation, power, recognition, and position than it does about his holy honor. *In your responses, whose honor, glory, and position are you seeking to defend?*

• *I will live within my God-designed limits (Rom. 12:3).* I am not frustrated by my limits because I really do believe that God is present with me, actively delivering to me everything I need in order to be what he has chosen me to be and to do the things he has called me to do and in the way he has chosen me to do them. Why would you ever be discouraged by your limits when God hasn't left you to your little bag of resources, but is constantly supplying you with things that you would never have without the generosity of his presence and grace? So, I am freed from trying to do what I have no power to do. I am freed from asking the harshness of my words or the threat of my dismissal or the force of my anger or the power of my tribe to do what only God, in his infinite power and amazing grace, can do. *In your reactions, do you step outside your limits, trying to create in others what you have no power to create?*

- *I will remember that my world is not out of control (Acts 17:22–34).* I love the apostle Paul's response to the Athenian philosophers, as he defined for them the God they thought they could not know. He talks of God's control, saying that God determines the exact length of our lives and the exact places where we live (17:26). But then he says something that is hugely comforting. Paul says that God does this so that he will be near to each one of us so that, at any moment, we can reach out and touch him (17:27). God is not just sovereign over everything; he is *sovereignly present.* His sovereignty guarantees his presence and his presence guarantees that our worlds are never out of control. If I believe in his presence and rule, then I am freed from reacting out of panic, out of the need for control, or as a play for power of my own. Life is not about gaining as much power and control as you can, but rather about resting in the one who has unstoppable power over everything in heaven and on earth. *Does the way I react to others demonstrate the wisdom, power, and presence of the one who holds all things under his control?*

✳

As I was working on this final chapter of this book, I was talking with Luella, my partner in everything, about the beauty of living with a recognition of the presence of the Lord, and she said, "Be still, and know that I am God" (Ps. 46:10). As she walked away, I grabbed my phone and googled Psalm 46. I called her back and told her that she had given me the ending for this book. She responded, "I was just praying that God would give you just the right ending." Yes, he is present. He does care. He does answer prayer. He does supply what we need. He is good, gracious, and generous. His holiness never contradicts his love. His power never crushes his tender grace. In one moment on one morning, Luella and I learned again that he is with us in tenderly responsive grace.

So we end with Psalm 46. The worldview of this psalm is the backdrop for everything in this book. In a world of chaos, with people raging, we do not need to fear for one reason and one reason alone: God is God. Take time to luxuriate in this wonderful psalm. Give it time not just to inform you but more importantly to transform you. You see, being still and remembering that God is God is not about denying the troubling realities of the fallen world that you live in. These realities are graphically depicted throughout this psalm. No, being still and knowing that God is God is about what controls your conscious and not-so conscious meditation. Rather than spending so much time going from site to site tracing how messed up people and your world are, perhaps it would be better to invest more time bathing your soul in the invigorating waters of the glory of God. And as you do that, remind yourself that all that God is, he is for you, by grace.

God is our refuge and strength,
a very present help in trouble.
Therefore we will not fear though the earth gives way,
though the mountains be moved into the heart of the sea,

though its waters roar and foam,
    though the mountains tremble at its swelling.   *Selah*
There is a river whose streams make glad the city of God,
    the holy habitation of the Most High.
God is in the midst of her; she shall not be moved;
    God will help her when morning dawns.
The nations rage, the kingdoms totter;
    he utters his voice, the earth melts.
The LORD of hosts is with us;
    the God of Jacob is our fortress.   *Selah*
Come, behold the works of the LORD,
    how he has brought desolations on the earth.
He makes wars cease to the end of the earth;
    he breaks the bow and shatters the spear;
    he burns the chariots with fire.
"Be still, and know that I am God.
    I will be exalted among the nations,
    I will be exalted in the earth!"
The LORD of hosts is with us;
    the God of Jacob is our fortress.   *Selah* (Ps. 46)

Perhaps radical change would take place in the often toxic environment of the Christian community and of the world of Christian social media if all of us, responding to the call of Psalm 46, spent much more time *being still.*

General Index

Ps 143.8
Let the morning
bring me word of your
unfailing love,
for I have put my trust in you.
Show me the way I should go
for you I entrust my life

Isaiah 54 "Though the mountains
be shaken
and the hills be removed,
yet my unfailing love for
you will not be shaken
nor my covenant of peace
be moved,"
Says the Lord, who has
compassion on you.
Sing - burst into song - shout for Joy
more are the children of the
desolate women than other ---
Maker is _your husband_
Holy one y<u>our</u> redeemer
God of all the earth
Called back with deep
-Everlasting kindness-   compassion

Isaiah 26:3 Peace ___ Replace
                                        Fear
               Trust ___
               Gratitude   Plans
               ♡ Foundation   hope
Seek   +
God's   future
of Love/ Shift from ___   not to
         to promise   harm

Scripture Index

Isa 43:19 Something New will spring forth, will you not be aware of it

Proverbs 16:9 Man plans his way Lord directs his steps

I will even make a roadway in wilder Jeremiah ch 29:11 ness Rivers (in deserts) 31:17 Plans to give you hope and a future hopeful future

All that God has prepared for those who Love Him

I Corinthians 2:9 eye ear not entered thee

Also Available from Paul David Tripp

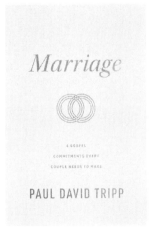